READY-TO-USE RESOURCES FOR

GRIT IN THE CLASSROOM

Ready-to-Use Resources for Grit in the Classroom provides tools to help teachers, students, and families understand and foster passionate, creative, and curious grit in all students.

It can be difficult and time consuming to figure out how to develop grit in the classroom. This resource includes student activities and mini-lessons that can be completed in fewer than ten minutes, with activities on topics from goal setting, to re-examining failure, to optimism. Interactive and engaging, this book challenges students to rethink failure, push past obstacles, and passionately pursue their interests.

Featuring helpful teacher instructions and reproducible handouts for each activity, *Ready-to-Use Resources for Grit in the Classroom* is the perfect addition to any educator's social-emotional learning library.

Laila Y. Sanguras is a former middle school teacher with a Ph.D. in educational research. A recipient of the 2021 Outstanding Teaching award from Baylor University, she is passionate about supporting teachers and students at every level.

T0347184

READY-TO-USE RESOURCES FOR

GRIT IN THE CLASSROOM

ACTIVITIES AND MINI-LESSONS FOR BUILDING PASSION AND PERSEVERANCE

Laila Y. Sanguras

Routledge
Taylor & Francis Group

NEW YORK AND LONDON

READY-TO-USE RESOURCES FOR

GRIT IN THE CLASSROOM

Cover image: @Shutterstock

First published 2022
by Routledge
605 Third Avenue, New York, NY 10158

and by Routledge
4 Park Square, Milton Park, Abingdon, Oxon, OX14 4RN

Routledge is an imprint of the Taylor & Francis Group, an informa business

Library of Congress Cataloging-in-Publication Data
A catalog record for this title has been requested

ISBN: 978-1-032-14506-8 (hbk)
ISBN: 978-1-64632-217-6 (pbk)
ISBN: 978-1-003-23761-7 (ebk)

DOI: 10.4324/9781003237617

Typeset in Helvetica
by Newgen Publishing UK

Contents

Acknowledgments

Thank you, Micah Benson, for creating the images and illustrations.

GRIT IN THE CLASSROOM

Welcome

With the increased emphasis on developing the social-emotional skills of students in the past decade, *grit* has become a popular buzzword. It is often used synonymously with *perseverance* and *stick-to-it-iveness*, without the equal attention paid to passion and curiosity. This resource book provides the tools needed to help teachers, students, and families understand that grit is two-faceted, and that both facets are crucial to grow.

Most people who work with students want them to have grit (i.e., passion and perseverance), but it can be difficult and time consuming to figure out exactly how to develop these psychosocial skills. In fact, when I was working with a group of teachers a few years ago, they loved everything I had to say about grit, but really needed to know *how* to cultivate their students' passion and perseverance. Specifically, they wanted resources they could use in their classrooms tomorrow. Well, being a people pleaser who never misses an opportunity, I immediately got to work and created this book just for them (and you)! This resource book includes specific activities that can be completed in fewer than 10 minutes, along with direct instructions for how teachers can support their students for each activity.

I have combined my expertise on grit and my creativity in lesson development to create this book. The student activities range from goal setting to re-examining how we view failure, in addition to calendar space for students to track their assignments and their progression toward their goals.

A note on the organization of this resource book: The resources are organized by topic and are not meant to be completed in order from cover to cover. A recommended order of activities is included in the appendix.

Enjoy!

DOI: 10.4324/9781003237617-1

GRIT IN THE CLASSROOM

Introduction

What is Grit?

Angela Duckworth (2016), a professor and researcher, has become the name associated with grit. She defined *grit* as sustained perseverance coupled with intense passion. According to Duckworth, people can be successful if they persevere through challenges and are passionate about their pursuit.

In a 2016 *Fortune* 500 Insiders Network forum, Greg Hyslop, the chief technology officer of The Boeing Company, made the case that perseverance is the most important skill a millennial can have. Hyslop argued that most of Boeing's projects could take a decade or more to complete, but that many younger employees will not stick around to their completion. Those who stay with a project long term learn the problem solving and conflict management skills that are critical to being successful in innovative fields. Those who quit and move onto the next shiny object miss out on those skills. Grit involves *sustained* perseverance.

However, grit can *only* exist when sustained perseverance is paired with passion (Duckworth, 2016). Passion is a strong desire for an activity, object, or person that one loves, values, and invests time and energy into. It is the "why" that gets us out of bed in the morning, and it is crucial that we help our students find their "why."

In building grit, effort counts twice – more than achievement and more than talent (Duckworth, 2016). As teachers who give our students everything we have (and then some), we can take practical steps toward cultivating grit in our students. When we place an emphasis on effort, authentic effort, with our students, we are also showing them a way to improve their performance.

I also want to take a moment to acknowledge that many students live in conditions that seem to naturally breed grit. You may have students who have adult responsibilities or who live in poverty or who attend schools that are under-resourced. Those students are often described as being gritty. In fact, there are some people out there who use grit as an actual reason to *not* address the issues of kids having adult responsibilities or living in poverty or attending under-resourced schools (Ris, 2015). They say that these conditions are actually making them stronger and more likely to be overcome future obstacles. Ummm, excuse me? This reasoning is completely ludicrous and those people should be uninvited to the conversations about how to support students and improve schools. This is not the context in which I discuss grit in this book. Before we do anything to address the academic and social development of students, we must first address issues that create inequitable educational experiences for our children (Stokas, 2015). Every child deserves a first-class education delivered by teachers who are appropriately compensated for their time, energy, and expertise. Period.

You Are a Hope Dealer

Let's face it. Asking students to rethink failure, push past obstacles, and passionately pursue their interests are great expectations. These are difficult and messy things we are asking our students to do, but we know that these are the keys to helping them lead happy, successful lives.

That being said, it is important that you know your role. I know, I know; you already do a million things, but this is crucial. You are a Hope Dealer. This means that you need to be the one standing right by each student as they mentally refocus their attention from their failure to what they can learn and how they can improve from that experience. You must help your students recognize the obstacles that are already present in their lives, and help them shift those obstacles to opportunities.

You can provide hope through words of encouragement, smiles, and showing your students that you are on this journey with them. You can also share your own experiences with overcoming obstacles, failures, and successes. Not only can you be an example of what it means to be gritty, your willingness to be vulnerable further opens the door to deep connections with your students.

You've Got This

You can read more about the importance of cultivating grit in my books *Grit in the Classroom: Building Perseverance for Excellence in Today's Students* and *Raising Children with Grit: Parenting Passionate, Persistent, and Successful Students*.

GRIT IN THE CLASSROOM

Chapter 1: How Gritty Am I?

Raise your hand if you love taking quizzes – if you have taken the "how good a friend are you" quiz or the "what Harry Potter house do you belong in" quiz or "what kind of cheese are you" quiz. Well, I am right there with you. I take these quizzes because I am curious about the answers, but also because I want to see how the quiz creator is going to determine a quiz based on a few personality questions. Once I started learning about designing assessments, I learned that my curiosity actually stems from trying to determine how a construct is measured.

Think about this. If you were handed a bunch of questions related to balancing equations, you could probably deduce that you were holding an algebra quiz. Your brain is working to put the pieces together to provide a context for these questions. This is why I think it is important to really dive into the grit scale when we first start discussing grit with students. We can learn a lot about what it means to be gritty simply by reading the items that measure grittiness.

In this chapter, students will take Duckworth's grit scale and explore the different dimensions of what it means to be gritty. There are seven specific activities included:

1. The Grit Quiz
2. GRIT Acrostic
3. SWOT Analysis
4. SWOT Review
5. Grit and Growth Mindset
6. Owning Your Power
7. Changes in Grit

DOI: 10.4324/9781003237617-3

THIS IS MOSTLY TRUE ABOUT ME . . .

THIS IS MOSTLY UNTRUE ABOUT ME . . .

Laila Y. Sanguras 2022, *Ready-to-Use Resources for Grit in the Classroom*, Routledge

The Grit Quiz

Before diving into the activities in this book of resources, it is important that we help students understand what grit is. One of the best ways to do this is to really look at the items used to measure grit. Tell students that we want to see how gritty they are. They should answer each question honestly; be sure to explain that there are no right or wrong answers.

You can have students complete Duckworth's grit scale directly on her website (https://angeladuckworth.com/research/). You can select from the 12-Item Grit-O Scale (Duckworth et al., 2007) and the 8-Item Grit-S Scale (Duckworth & Quinn, 2009), depending on what you think will be best for your students. The directions for scoring the instrument are provided at the end of each quiz. At the top of the "How Gritty Are You?" page, ask students to write their total grit scores. Then they also need to choose the two items that are MOST like them and write those in the top box. They will write the two items that are most NOT like them and write those in the bottom box. You can tell them that you will revisit this later in the year.

It is also a good idea to talk through each item after students complete the quiz. I suggest that you write each question on the board and then talk through it with your students. For example, one item is "I have overcome setbacks to conquer an important challenge." You might ask students to share times when they or someone they know has overcome setbacks. You might ask them to explain how it felt to overcome setbacks or how they know the difference between an important challenge and a not-so-important challenge.

WHAT DOES GRIT
MEAN TO YOU?

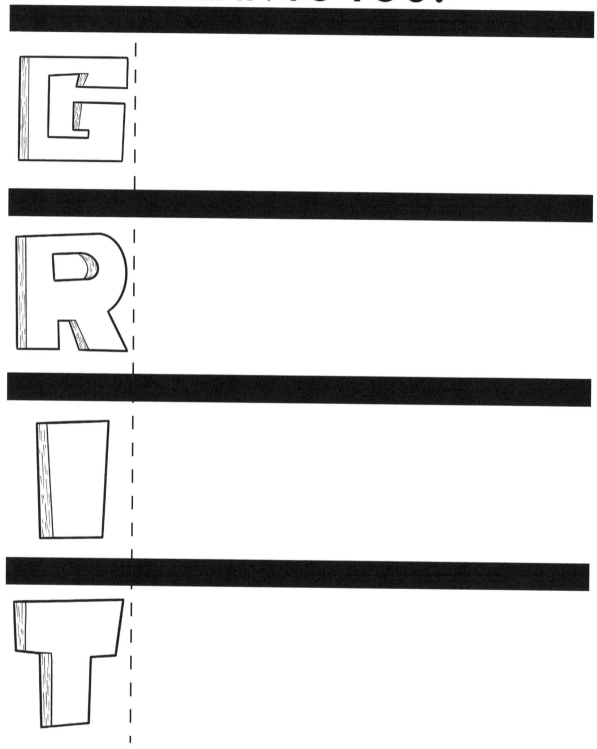

Laila Y. Sanguras 2022, *Ready-to-Use Resources for Grit in the Classroom*, Routledge

GRIT Acrostic

Ask students about the two components to grit (passion and perseverance) and remind them that both are important. Explain that passion is what keeps us moving when we want to give up and that everyone who has ever accomplished something great wanted to quit at some point. Also explain that perseverance is when we can see the obstacles, but we choose to keep going anyway. Perseverance is what gets us to reach our goals, while it is the passion that keeps us moving forward.

Give students time to complete the GRIT acrostic poem. They need to start each sentence with each letter in the word "grit." They can add additional sentences to explain themselves when necessary and can include examples. Students can also add drawings/images that coincide with each letter. You can have students present their poems to the class or in small groups. You also might consider displaying these in your classroom.

Think deeply about how you would describe these aspects of your identity.

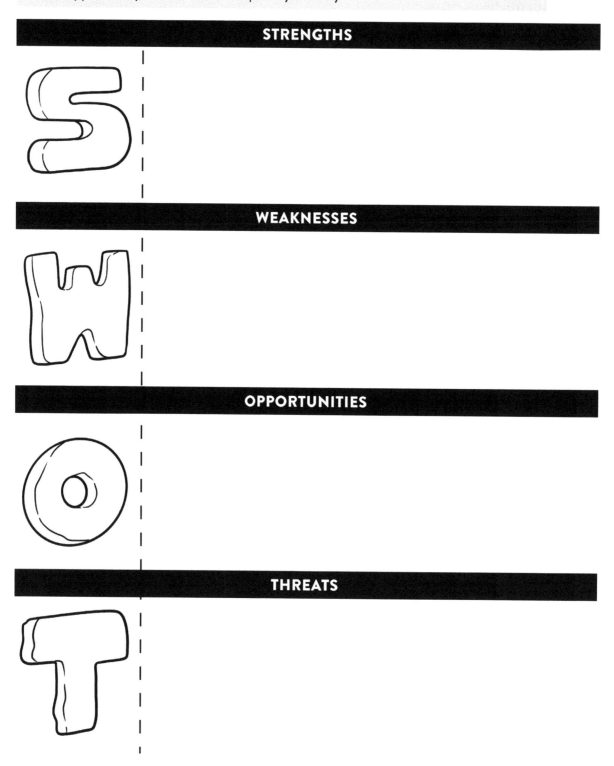

STRENGTHS

WEAKNESSES

OPPORTUNITIES

THREATS

Laila Y. Sanguras 2022, *Ready-to-Use Resources for Grit in the Classroom*, Routledge

SWOT Analysis

An important component to being gritty is knowing who we are. We need to have a strong sense of our identity and a SWOT (Strengths, Weaknesses, Opportunities, and Threats) analysis can help (Pestle Analysis Contributor, 2015)! Begin first by modeling your own SWOT analysis for your students and then lead them through their own. Depending on your students, this might be something they can work on with a partner or alone.

Students will identify their personal strengths, weaknesses, opportunities (the resources they have available to them), and threats (things that might hinder them). You may need to coax students to really think about their strengths. For example, they sometimes do not realize that being bilingual or being immersed in two different cultures is a positive thing. The same is true for opportunities. For some, they may have financial stability in their family, which is an obvious opportunity. For others, they may have a lot of siblings (which seems like a pain), but is actually a resource because they always have people around them. (This SWOT analysis is a really great one to talk through individually with students who are struggling in your class, are not motivated, etc. It is a great tool to help you connect to them.)

SWOT REVIEW

WHAT ARE ADDITIONAL STRENGTHS YOU HAVE?

WHAT IS A WEAKNESS THAT YOU WANT TO IMPROVE? WHAT CAN YOU DO TO TURN IT INTO A STRENGTH?

WHAT OPPORTUNITY DO YOU FEEL WILL HELP YOU THE MOST?

HOW CAN YOU TURN ONE OF YOUR THREATS INTO STRENGTHS?

Laila Y. Sanguras 2022, *Ready-to-Use Resources for Grit in the Classroom*, Routledge

SWOT Review

The SWOT Review is an activity to complete at the end of a semester or school year. We want to provide students with the opportunity to reflect and connect back to their initial SWOT analysis.

You might begin this activity by displaying your own SWOT analysis and completing your review in front of your students. This could provide some ideas for how they can answer each of the reflective questions. Students can continue the reflection process by sharing with a partner or small group.

Grit and Growth Mindset

Growth mindset is the belief that effort and time result in higher achievement, and that we are in control of our success (Dweck, 2007). Sounds similar to grit, doesn't it? The opposite of a growth mindset, fixed mindset, is when we believe we are just not smart/talented/gifted enough and that is all there is to it. Grit and growth mindset are obviously closely related, so I have curated three golden rules for how to cultivate grit by operating a growth mindset.

As you walk through each of the three golden rules, students can take notes around the words about what this means to them:

1. We work hard every day. That means that every single day we are giving everything we have. We do not complain about the work we are given because we know it is necessary to succeed.
2. We practice optimism. This means that we are going to believe in ourselves, even when things get hard. We know that life is going to throw us curve balls, but we believe that if we keep moving forward, things will get better. We shut down the voice in our heads that says we cannot do something.
3. We own our power. We have the power to be engaged and interested and motivated. Our teachers can work super hard to develop creative lessons, but it is up to us to engage our brains and be active participants in our learning.

OWN YOUR POWER

How can you show others that you are focused on achieving your super stretch goals?

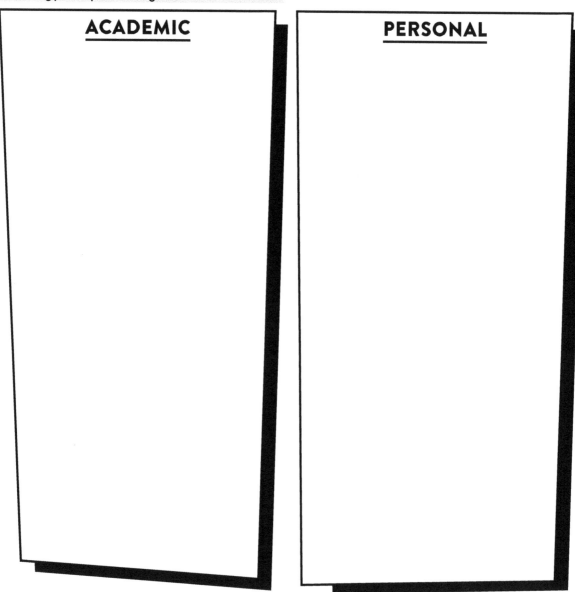

ACADEMIC

PERSONAL

Owning Your Power

It is time to ask students to think back on their academic and personal Super Stretch Goals (SSGs). Also, remind students that the key to having a growth mindset and grit is that we own our power – WE are in charge of how hard we work and how much time we put into achieving our goals.

Ask students to write down actions they can take in each column to show others that they are focused on their goals. For example, someone focused on getting As in their classes, might write "I spend at least 30-minutes every night reading or doing homework" in the Academic column. You can brainstorm and share how you own your power as you pursue your professional and personal goals. What exactly do you do and what does that look like? You might ask students to share their actions with a partner or small group.

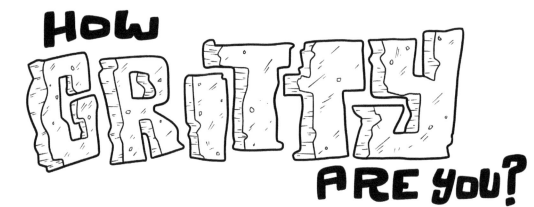

How has your grit score changed?

How has your thinking changed about your ability to persevere?

How have your passions changed?

Changes in Grit

At the end of the semester or school year, ask students to go back and take the Grit-O Scale (Duckworth et al., 2007) or Grit-S Scale (Duckworth & Quinn, 2009) again. It is important that students take the same version that they took at the beginning of the year. Just as before, students need to respond to each question honestly and not worry about getting them right or wrong.

Then provide students with time to think about how their interests and their thoughts on perseverance have changed. In each box, students will respond to the questions. This is another great opportunity for a conversation with a partner.

Chapter 2: Goal Setting

When I was a teacher, we started each year with goal setting. I remember that we typically had a goal assigned to us by the district that usually had something to do with a district initiative and a goal assigned to us by the campus that usually had something to do with achievement scores. We also set a third goal that we could identify for ourselves. Now, first of all, it makes little sense to me why a district or campus would assign a goal for a teacher. (Hello, zero buy-in or commitment.)

Second, there was a problem in how we went about pursuing these goals. In short, we didn't. We set the goals at the beginning of the year. Then we revisited them at the end of the year. Each teacher had to present proof of achieving each goal, which left us scrambling for test scores or other evidence that we could share. The goals were not our focus for the year, probably because we were too busy putting out the day-to-day fires to think about what the district wanted from us.

This brings me to the third problem of this process. None of the goals that we were asked to set were light-up-your-eyes-set-your-belly-on-fire goals. They were SMART (specific, measurable, attainable, realistic, and timely) goals (Doran, 1981). Now, while there is absolutely the right time for a SMART goal, the beginning of the year is not that time. The beginning of the year is when we should be dreaming big, scary goals because these are the things that will keep us focused on improving our craft.

In this chapter, students will practice how to set academic and personal Super Stretch Goals, SMART goals, and daily actions. There are nine student activities included:

1. Weekly Calendar
2. Super Stretch Goals
3. Breaking Down the Academic Super Stretch Goal
4. Evaluating the Academic Super Stretch Goal
5. Breaking Down the Personal Super Stretch Goal
6. Evaluating the Personal Super Stretch Goal
7. I Did It!
8. Feeling Like a Winner
9. My Future is Bright

DOI: 10.4324/9781003237617-4

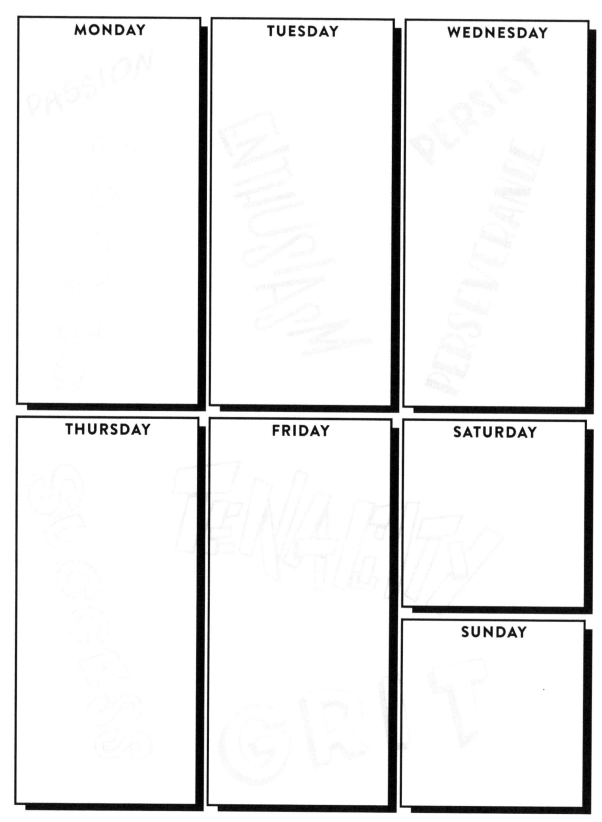

MONDAY	TUESDAY	WEDNESDAY

THURSDAY	FRIDAY	SATURDAY
		SUNDAY

Weekly Calendar

The weekly calendar pages are for you to distribute to students as needed. Explain that the purpose of keeping a calendar is to anticipate obstacles that may get in the way of meeting their commitments (and to make sure they do not forget anything). The weekly calendar is an opportunity to look through a telescope to zoom into a week within the month. However, it is crucial that you regularly provide the time it takes to add in their weekly commitments. If we value this process (and we do), we have to provide the few minutes it takes to complete the activity together. It is also important that you model this process until they get the hang of it. You likely will have students who prefer a digital calendar, and this is totally fine. The purpose is accomplished regardless of medium.

Once students have added commitments to their weekly calendars, model how they can anticipate potential barriers that may get in their way. For example, you can walk through your weekly commitments and identify points in the week that may keep you from meeting those commitments. (For example, if you have grades due on Friday, but back-to-back meetings on Thursday, talk through how you can block out time on Wednesday to work on your grades.)

WHAT'S MY SUPER STRETCH GOAL?

A Super Stretch Goal is your ultimate dream. It's something that you might be scared to write down, but it is exciting to think about happening.

ACADEMIC

PERSONAL

Laila Y. Sanguras 2022, *Ready-to-Use Resources for Grit in the Classroom*, Routledge

Super Stretch Goals

A Super Stretch Goal is a dream that you have for your life. It can be scary to talk about and write down, but it is also exciting to think about. Share a personal and professional Super Stretch Goal you have for yourself. Maybe you want to be named Disney's American Teacher or meet the President. Or maybe you want to run a marathon or write a book. Whatever it is, show your students how to dream by sharing your Super Stretch Goals.

Give students time to brainstorm Super Stretch Goals that fall into each bucket. Encourage them to dream – the sky is the limit. Help them by providing some ideas (get a full scholarship to college, make the high school basketball team, etc.). They can list as many as they can imagine. Encourage them to continue thinking about these dreams and let them know that they can return to this page to add to each bucket.

WHAT'S MY ACADEMIC SUPER STRETCH GOAL?

SMART GOALS

DAILY ACTIONS

Laila Y. Sanguras 2022, *Ready-to-Use Resources for Grit in the Classroom*, Routledge

Breaking Down the Academic Super Stretch Goal

This activity is designed to have students choose an Academic Super Stretch Goal from the list they brainstormed earlier and then create a plan for making it happen. First, explain the difference between a Super Stretch Goal (also called a dream) and a SMART (specific, measurable, achievable, relevant, and timely) goal (Doran, 1981). (You can learn more about SMART goals here: www.mindtools.com/pages/article/smart-goals.htm.)

I also suggest that you model this with your own professional SSG. Have students write down their Super Stretch Goal (SSG) and then write three SMART goals that lead to the SSG. As they are working, give feedback on their goals. From there, they need to write down three daily actions that align with each SMART goal. This means they will have one SSG, three SMART goals, and nine daily actions by the end of the activity. The actions are things they can do every day to get them closer to accomplishing their SMART goals. Once they are done, have them walk through their goals and actions with a partner. The partner can provide feedback on their goals and actions.

This is an example of a personal SSG from *Raising Children with Grit: Parenting Passionate, Persistent, and Successful Kids* (Sanguras, 2018).

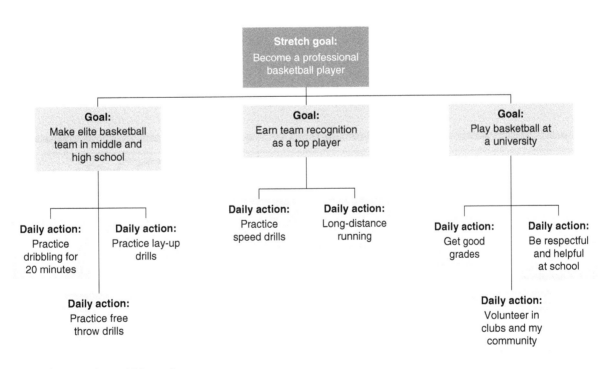

Example stretch goal hierarchy

— ROBERT COLLIER

ACADEMIC SMART GOAL

Daily Actions	Rate your success from 1 (not so great) to 10 (nailed it).	Start, stop, continue, change

SMART Goal Achieved?

Laila Y. Sanguras 2022, *Ready-to-Use Resources for Grit in the Classroom*, Routledge

Evaluating the Academic Super Stretch Goal

This activity should be completed at the end of a semester or school year. Robert Collier (2009), an author, said, "Success is the sum of small efforts repeated day in and day out." Talk through the quote with your students. Ask them what Collier means and how his message relates to grit.

You can model this activity for your students. In the first column, they need to write down the daily actions that they identified in the "Breaking Down the Academic SSG" activity. In the middle column, they will rate their success at doing that action daily over the past few months. They will rate each action. In the last column, they will write whether they are going to start this daily action (because they did not actually start it before), stop the action (because it does not seem to be getting them closer to their SSG), continue the action (because they are doing a great job with it), or change the action (because they need to do something differently). At the bottom of the page, they will circle the thumbs up if they achieved their SSG or the thumbs down if they did not. (Remind students that there is nothing wrong with not achieving the goal – if it is a big one, it is going to take a while to get there.) You can model this with your own academic/professional SSG.

WHAT'S MY PERSONAL SUPER STRETCH GOAL?

SMART GOALS

DAILY ACTIONS

Laila Y. Sanguras 2022, *Ready-to-Use Resources for Grit in the Classroom*, Routledge

Breaking Down the Personal Super Stretch Goal

In this activity, students will choose a Personal Super Stretch Goal and then create a plan for making it happen. Remind them of the difference between a Super Stretch Goal (also called a dream) and a SMART (specific, measurable, achievable, relevant, and timely) goal.

You can model this with your own personal SSG. Have students take their Super Stretch Goal (SSG) and then write three SMART goals that lead to the SSG. As they are working, give feedback on their goals. From there, they need to write down three daily actions that align with each SMART goal. This means they will have one SSG, three SMART goals, and nine daily actions by the end of the activity. The actions are things they can do every day to get them closer to accomplishing their SMART goals. Once they are done, have students walk through their goals and actions with a partner. The partner should give them feedback on their goals and actions.

—RYAN LOWRY

PERSONAL SMART GOAL

Daily Actions	Rate your success from 1 (not so great) to 10 (nailed it).	Start, stop, continue, change

SMART Goal Achieved?

Laila Y. Sanguras 2022, *Ready-to-Use Resources for Grit in the Classroom*, Routledge

Evaluating the Personal Super Stretch Goal

I was listening to a health podcast (Gregory, 2020) one day and heard the guest Dr. Ryan Lowery say, "It's a long process, but quitting won't speed it up." He was referring to making health improvements, but this quote really applies to anything that takes time to accomplish. Talk through the quote. What do they think Lowery means? What is "it?"

This activity is the same as Evaluating the Academic SSG. You can model this activity for your students. In the first column, they need to write down the daily actions that they identified in the "Breaking Down the Personal SSG" activity. In the middle column, they will rate their success at doing that action daily over the past few months. They will rate each action. In the last column, they will write whether they are going to start this daily action (because they did not actually start it before), stop the action (because it does not seem to be getting them closer to their SSG), continue the action (because they are doing a great job with it), or change the action (because they need to do something differently). At the bottom of the page, they will circle the thumbs up if they achieved their SSG or the thumbs down if they did not. (Remind students that there is nothing wrong with not achieving the goal – if it is a big one, it is going to take a while to get there.)

I DID IT!

1. _____

2. _____

3. _____

4. _____

5. _____

Laila Y. Sanguras 2022, *Ready-to-Use Resources for Grit in the Classroom*, Routledge

I Did It!

At the end of each semester, take time to help students celebrate their accomplishments. Have students write down five things they have accomplished that make them feel proud – these can be personal or academic. Encourage them to think about the daily actions they defined and the SMART goals they set – maybe one thing from the list can be that they kept their daily commitments or that they got closer to their SSGs. This is a great opportunity for you to provide them with time to share their accomplishments – they could announce them to the class, add them to a bulletin board, etc.

Laila Y. Sanguras 2022, *Ready-to-Use Resources for Grit in the Classroom*, Routledge

Feeling Like a Winner

We want to also provide students to reflect on how it feels to win or accomplish something. Does it make them feel proud? Happy? Inside each trophy, students will write down a feeling they have when they win. Encourage students to be creative in their word choice, maybe even use a thesaurus. The point is that we want them to be able to articulate their feelings, good and bad, as they go about their daily activities.

Next year I will . . .

1. _____

2. _____

3. _____

Laila Y. Sanguras 2022, *Ready-to-Use Resources for Grit in the Classroom*, Routledge

My Future is Bright

The end of the school year is a great time to start thinking about SSGs for the next school year. These can be the same or different from the ones they set this year. The point is that we want them to reflect on their progress AND to have a sense of the things they want to continue to pursue. We want students to have a clear understanding of what drives them.

Ask students to write down three Super Stretch Goals that they have for themselves next year. These can be a combination of personal and academic. Remind students that these are big, scary dreams that will take a lot of passion and perseverance (GRIT!) to accomplish.

Chapter 3: Cultivating Curiosity

In my time working with teachers, I have realized that we have a curiosity catastrophe on our hands. Hear me out … We know that children are naturally curious and FULL of questions (Kettle & Ross, 2018). But they slowly recognize that as they get older, curiosity is no longer valued (Archer et al., 2017). There is no longer time to talk about whether a ladybug has a family or what a dog dreams about because we have objectives to meet and lessons to finish. But this is a problem, folks.

I first realized the problem when I was teaching eighth grade. As the language arts teacher, I would trade places with the science teacher during Science Fair time. I would go into her science classes and work with students as they wrote up their reports. She would go into my language arts classes and work on something sciency. I was SO excited. I walked around and asked students why they chose their topics. I mean, I couldn't imagine anything better than getting to pick any topic, design an experiment, and then see what happened! More often than not, when I asked students why they chose their topics, they shrugged and said some version of, "I couldn't think of anything else" or "I thought this would be easy." Y'all, there was no passion or commitment – just the glazed eyes of a 13-year-old trying to make it through the class with minimal engagement. This is when I determined that we needed to do something about this.

In this chapter, students will be asked to participate in a variety of activities that push them to be curious. These activities are the basis for identifying potential passions. There are five activities focused on cultivating curiosity:

1. I Wonder …
2. I Used to Wonder …
3. Did You Know?
4. Research Ideas
5. My Inquiring Mind

DOI: 10.4324/9781003237617-5

1. _____

2. _____

3. _____

4. _____

5. _____

6. _____

7. _____

8. _____

9. _____

10. _____

I Wonder …

Remind students that an important component of grit is passion, and that we have to dedicate time to cultivating passion. Curiosity is what leads to interest which is what leads to passion (Warley, 2016), but we often don't spend time practicing curiosity. You can even talk to them about what it's like to be around younger siblings or if they are ever around kids who are 2 or 3 years old – they ask A LOT of questions. But then we tend to stop looking around at the world and wondering things. Sometimes this is because we learn that our questions aren't appreciated; other times it's because we are too immersed in our technology to notice the world around us. Tell them that over the course of the year we are going to practice the act of wondering.

Before doing this with your students, write your own I Wonder list of ten things that you can share with them. These can be related to work ("I wonder how I can motivate my students to read more?") or personal ("I wonder how I can get my dogs to stop barking at everyone who walks by my house?") or silly ("I wonder why off-brand cola loses its fizz faster than the name brand Coca-Cola or Pepsi?"). Give your students time to write down ten things they wonder about. If they cannot get all ten written down before you are ready to move on, tell them that they can come back to this page to complete it throughout the week. Also, remind them that you will be regularly requiring them to wonder throughout the year so they should be paying attention to the world around them. If they think of something to wonder, they can write it down and save it for the next time you complete this activity.

I encourage you to build in "I wonder" time at the beginning of each week. Students can keep a running list so that next time they need a topic for something to study/investigate/research/write about, they have a list of potential topics. If they know that you expect them to write five "I wonder" statements every Monday at the beginning of the day, they will start to train their brains to "wonder," simply in preparation for Monday's task.

I USED TO WONDER...

AND NOW I KNOW...

Laila Y. Sanguras 2022, *Ready-to-Use Resources for Grit in the Classroom*, Routledge

I Used to Wonder ...

We want to empower students to look for the answers to the questions they have. To begin, ask students to look back at their "I Wonder" lists they generated earlier. Have them choose two to three and write them in the top box. Then, give students time to research those topics briefly. In the bottom box they will write what they now know about each "wonder" from the top box. Essentially, they are turning a wonder into a fun fact. Encourage them to share.

Like the "I Wonder" activity, this is also one that you can return to again and again. Remember that we want students to continue to revisit this idea and to build their wonderment by cycling through old and new ideas constantly. We want to turn their brains into little idea factories.

DID YOU KNOW?!

1. _____

2. _____

3. _____

4. _____

5. _____

6. _____

7. _____

8. _____

Laila Y. Sanguras 2022, *Ready-to-Use Resources for Grit in the Classroom*, Routledge

Did You Know?

Remind your students of the importance of curiosity and that you will be exploring their different interests throughout the year (with the hope that they can describe several things they are passionate about by the end of the year). In addition to practicing being curious, students also need to explore those curiosities and turn them into fun facts. For example, you can share this cute story about Polly, the goat with anxiety: www.thedodo.com/rescue-goat-duck-costume-2107301918.html (Alberts, 2016). That's quite a "did you know" story, right?

Ask students to write down eight fun facts about anything they want. These can be related to what they wrote down on the "I Wonder" brainstorm earlier or they can be completely different. They may have these fun facts in their heads already or they may need to do some research. An important thing to remember is that exposure to new ideas breeds new ideas – we want our students to generate ideas constantly, so they have to share. They can do this in a way that works best for you – you can post them to a bulletin board, create a space in your room to share ideas, use a hashtag (#didyouknow) and have students post to Twitter, or just talk about them. (They can search up those ideas by the hashtag later.) You could assign a student to be the weekly "Did You Know" generator and they are in charge of sharing three fun facts about anything they want with the class that week. The point is that we get students passionate about learning and intrigued by all of the things they don't know (but that are actually pretty cool).

IF I COULD RESEARCH ANYTHING
WHAT WOULD I

RESEARCH

1. _____

2. _____

3. _____

4. _____

5. _____

Laila Y. Sanguras 2022, *Ready-to-Use Resources for Grit in the Classroom*, Routledge

Research Ideas

We want to encourage students throughout the year to keep a list of their interests. My husband is also a professor and we both carry around "Idea Notebooks" which are little notebooks filled with … ideas! These are ideas for things we want to write about, questions we have, research topics, and so on. The notebooks are sometimes the tiny little spiral ones and sometimes nicer Moleskine ones. I know what you're wondering and yes, we are a blast at parties.

In this activity, have students think of five things they are interested in and write them down. Then they can meet in small groups to share their ideas. The point of sharing comes back to the concept that exposure to new ideas breeds new ideas. Encourage students to add to their lists if someone says something they also would like to research.

1. _____

2. _____

3. _____

Laila Y. Sanguras 2022, *Ready-to-Use Resources for Grit in the Classroom*, Routledge

My Inquiring Mind

This activity is designed to take students from the idea-generating stage to the research stage. We want them to look back at their "I Wonder" pages and select one topic. From there, they will write the topic in the box at the top of the page. Then they will research that topic and write down three interesting facts, hopefully addressing their wonderment. Of course, you can expand it from there. Students can then write an essay, create a presentation, and so on to generate a final product related to their topics.

Remember that exposure to new ideas breeds new ideas, so it is important that students share. However, I do remember my days as a classroom teacher when "Presentation Day" started out great and interesting, but then by the end I (and my students) were bored to tears and wondering when this torture would end. My tips are that you: 1) limit the amount of time for presentations (and carefully select a student to time them – you know the kind of kid I'm talking about), 2) present in small groups where you can rotate around to catch snippets of each presentation, 3) encourage multimedia presentations (i.e., including sound, video, etc.), and 4) no matter how old your students are, spend time discussing effective presentation techniques (i.e., limiting words on the slide and for the love of all things holy, please-do-not-read-to-us-what-we-can-read-ourselves-oh-my-gosh).

Chapter 4: Overcoming Obstacles

When I was a teacher, I was also a National Junior Honor Society sponsor. Over the years, I noticed an increase in students being reported to us for academic dishonesty. When I, full of righteousness and disappointment, would visit with these students I often left sad and understanding where they were coming from. You see, most of these high-achieving students were cheating for a pretty logical reason.

Ultimately, it came down to panic. When faced with the fact that they were unprepared for an assessment, students would do what needed to be done (which often meant copying a friend's work or looking up the answers during a test). Most of the students who described being unprepared explained that they had always excelled in this subject, but that it had gotten hard and they did not have the skills to study or figure things out. So they cheated. They also talked to me about how much their identity was wrapped up in being "the smart kid" and that they did not think they could handle it if their peers thought of them differently.

Picture it. If you have always been good at math, and then all of a sudden it gets hard, you might panic. You do not know what to do, first of all. Second, you do not want your identity as the smart kid to be rocked. Because if you are 13 and your sense of self is on the verge of being completely dismantled, you might do anything – even cheat – to save yourself. This is why I think we have to help students reimagine what it means to fail, we have to constantly challenge them so that they know how to recover from failure, and we have to help them tie their identities to the things that really matter (spoiler: what really matters is not the grade on a math test).

In this chapter, students will learn about successful/unsuccessful success and failure. They will reflect on times they have struggled and how they have persevered. Eleven activities are included in this section:

1. Challenges Faced
2. Self-Discipline
3. Obstacle Brainstorm
4. Moving On
5. Rethinking Failure
6. Productive and Unproductive Successes
7. Productive and Unproductive Failures
8. Distractions
9. Extrinsic Motivation
10. Intrinsic Motivation
11. Failure ≠ Self-Worth

DOI: 10.4324/9781003237617-6

Everyone who has ever done anything great has had to overcome obstacles, so we need to get used to the idea that we are going to struggle on the road to success. What are some challenges you have faced in your life? As you chase your dreams, what are the potential things that might get in your way?

Laila Y. Sanguras 2022, *Ready-to-Use Resources for Grit in the Classroom*, Routledge

Challenges Faced

"Struggle and success are a package." It is important that students understand that everyone who has ever done anything great has faced challenges. No one at the top of their field has gotten there without having to overcome some serious challenges. Share challenges you have faced throughout your life with your students. Not only will this bring authenticity to the activity, it will help students to know that you, a person they admire, has also had to overcome struggles.

In the space provided, students should write down any potential challenges that they have had to face AND any challenges that might get in the way of them being successful. For the first part, it might be that they struggled with reading in elementary school or their parents are divorced and they have the complication of splitting their time and belongings between two houses. For the second part, it might be finances or convincing their parents to sign them up for a special class or a competitive team. We want to acknowledge that struggles exist so that we can plan for them instead of being blindsided by them.

HOW DO I PRACTICE SELF-DISCIPLINE?

IN SCHOOL

OUTSIDE OF SCHOOL

Laila Y. Sanguras 2022, *Ready-to-Use Resources for Grit in the Classroom,* Routledge

Self-Discipline

Before beginning this activity, have a conversation with your students about what it means to have self-discipline – in both academic and personal areas of our lives. Sometimes self-discipline means that we must make the decision to stop watching a video so that we can do our homework. Or we might decide not to sit by a friend in class because we know we always talk instead of work. Other times it might mean that we choose not to drink soda because of the sugar and chemicals that are not helping us be our healthiest selves. Explain that self-discipline is important when it comes to building our grittiness. In fact, there is a positive relationship between grit and achievement (how well we do on tests), grades, school attendance, and study habits. In their research, Duckworth and Seligman (2005) found that the relationships between self-discipline and these other variables were higher than the relationship between IQ and those variables. Read that again because it is a fascinating statistic!

Ask your students to talk about how they practice self-discipline at school and outside of school. After this conversation, they can write down their reflections.

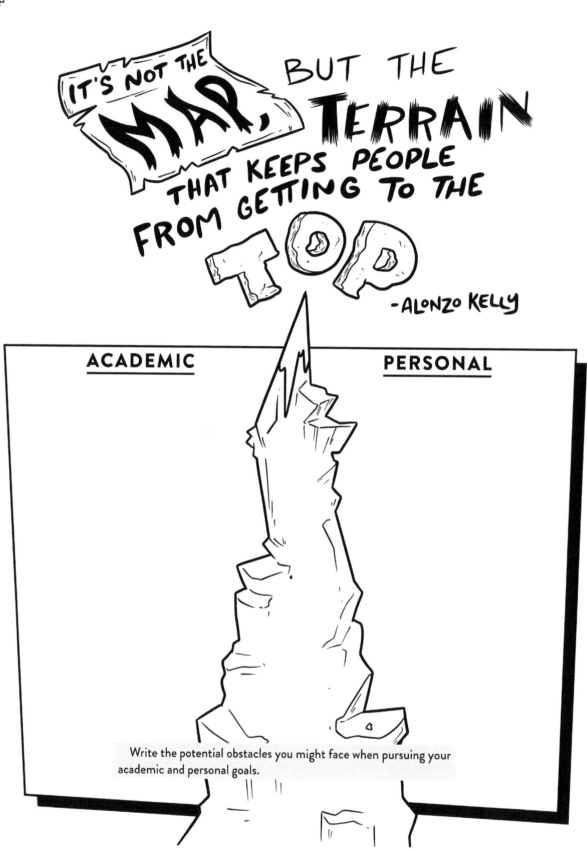

IT'S NOT THE MAP, BUT THE TERRAIN THAT KEEPS PEOPLE FROM GETTING TO THE TOP

—ALONZO KELLY

ACADEMIC

PERSONAL

Write the potential obstacles you might face when pursuing your academic and personal goals.

Laila Y. Sanguras 2022, *Ready-to-Use Resources for Grit in the Classroom*, Routledge

Obstacle Brainstorm

I was talking with Alonzo Kelly, a leadership coach and author, at a conference one day and he said, "It's not the map, but the terrain that keeps people from getting to the top." I remember thinking how much that relates to grit and I just had to write it down. Ask students what he means by "the terrain" and how this applies to our lives. Explain to students that obstacles are a part of life and will always be present. To be successful, we must figure out ways to overcome these obstacles. The first step is to identify what they are.

Ask students to brainstorm potential challenges they may face, things that might get in their way of achieving their academic and personal goals. Share possible ideas: lack of family support, not having enough money, bad grades, being out of shape, divorced parents, being unpopular, and so on. You can help them generate ideas by sharing obstacles that you have faced throughout your life, particularly those you faced when you were your students' ages.

YOU ARE EITHER REPAIRING YOUR PAST OR PREPARING YOUR FUTURE

- JOHN MAXWELL

Think about times in your life when you feel like you failed and list them in the space on the left. Be specific. Then think about how you moved on and describe it on the right. Again, be detailed.

TIMES I FELT LIKE I FAILED

HOW I MOVED ON

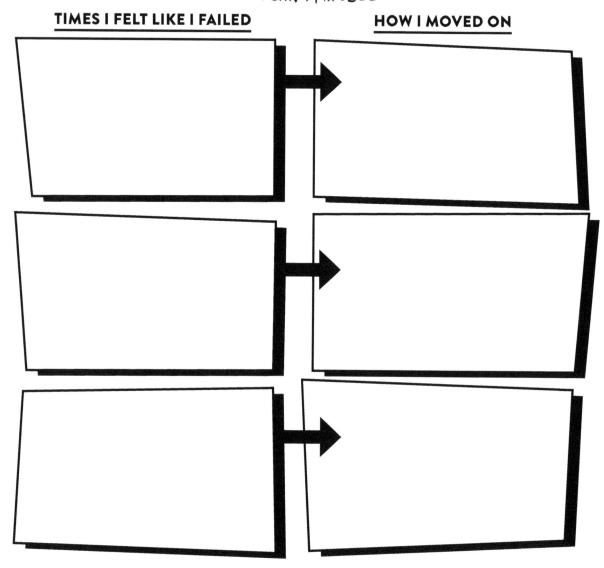

Moving On

To paraphrase John Maxwell (2011), an author and motivational speaker, "You are either repairing your past or preparing your future." Talk through this quote with your students. Explain that it means that we can either focus on the mistakes we have made, or we can focus on our goals and move forward. A failure, whatever that looks like, is just a data point – we do not need to spend time thinking about the failure or obsessing over all our mistakes. Instead, we need to see it as the point from which we can move forward. For example, instead of focusing on the fact that we failed a science quiz, we can plan for the next science quiz so that we can be more successful.

Ask students to think of three specific times that they felt like they failed at something. These failures can be academic or personal, big or small. They will describe each incident in the boxes on the left. On the right, they need to write down what they did to move on. In the science example, maybe they make a specific plan to study or go to tutoring. Help students brainstorm if they get stuck.

RETHINK failure

We've got to get comfortable with the uncomfortable. People, especially grown-ups, don't like to talk about failure. It makes us feel weak and full of shame, but we need to change all of that. We need to be able to think about times we've fallen short so that we can learn from those times and move forward. When you think about yourself and your life, what does it mean to fail? How do you feel when you fail?

Laila Y. Sanguras 2022, *Ready-to-Use Resources for Grit in the Classroom*, Routledge

Rethinking Failure

Chard Hurley, Steve Chen, and Jawed Karim were the founders of YouTube (Hosch, 2021). They took a lot of chances and, of course, encountered some setbacks. Their first office was above a pizzeria and, even if you love pizza, the smell got old pretty quickly. Plus, there were rats (yuck!) and they had to hang sheets from the ceiling to divide the large space into smaller working areas (before they were famous). They could have seen all of these things as reasons to give up, but they didn't. They kept pushing forward toward their goals.

Tell your students that they may not smell like pizza or they might not be living among rats, but they do have their own versions of failure. They need to think about how they define failure and then they can brainstorm what it means to fail in their lives. Is it getting a "B" on a report card? An "F?" Is it getting cut from the soccer team? Is it disappointing a parent? Is it being embarrassed in front of friends? Model what this means by sharing what it looks like for you to fail. Explain that this whole process is a part of getting comfortable with failing so that we do not give up when faced with a difficult situation. Also be clear that the failures they write down can be things they have experienced or things that they imagine. For example, I have never been fired from a job (knock on wood) but I would add this to my list of things that I would consider failures.

PRODUCTIVE SUCCESSES

UNPRODUCTIVE SUCCESSES

Laila Y. Sanguras 2022, *Ready-to-Use Resources for Grit in the Classroom*, Routledge

Productive and Unproductive Successes

At the top of this activity page, it says "Success is in the struggle." Talk through this with your students. Ask them to think about what it means to find success in the struggle. Then talk about the difference between something being productive and unproductive. A productive success is one in which you achieve your goal because you worked hard to get there (Kapur, 2016). For example, hitting a home run after hours of practice or finally understanding the math problem after working on it for a long time. An unproductive success is one in which you achieve your goal, but didn't really have to work hard to earn it. For example, earning a high grade in a class but knowing that you cheated or that you chose to take a class that was too easy for you. Or getting a trophy or medal just for signing up for a team, regardless of your ability or how hard you worked.

Next, students will write down productive and unproductive successes they have had in their lives. They can brainstorm with a partner or work individually. This is another opportunity that is great for sharing.

PRODUCTIVE FAILURES

UNPRODUCTIVE FAILURES

Laila Y. Sanguras 2022, *Ready-to-Use Resources for Grit in the Classroom*, Routledge

Productive and Unproductive Failures

In a previous activity, we talked about what it means to experience productive and unproductive successes, but we also have to talk about failures since we know they are inevitable. A productive failure is one in which you do not achieve your goal, but you benefit from the experience of trying (Kapur, 2016). Maybe your goal is to play professional tennis, but you do not actually make it to Wimbledon. But along the way, you played tennis in high school, earned scholarships to play in college, made friends, and kept in shape. An unproductive failure is one in which you do not achieve your goal and you do not learn anything from the process. Maybe you do not earn a good grade on a project – instead of learning and changing from the experience, you get mad and blame someone/something else for your grade.

Next, have students brainstorm their own productive and unproductive failures. You may need to coax them through the unproductive failure part, since it can be difficult to recognize when we have messed up (both in the act of not achieving the goal and in the process along the way).

WHAT ARE MY DISTRACTIONS

IN SCHOOL

OUTSIDE OF SCHOOL

Laila Y. Sanguras 2022, *Ready-to-Use Resources for Grit in the Classroom*, Routledge

Distractions

Distractions can get in the way of the things we want to accomplish. For example, in the process of writing this book, I have completely redone the landscaping in my front yard like I belong on one of those home improvement shows. (I do not belong on one, for the record.) To begin this activity, share some of your distractions that keep you from getting things done at home and at school.

Next, ask students to brainstorm a list of distractions that they face in school and outside of school. They can share in a short class discussion. Remember that it is important to identify the obstacles that could interfere with our success and, often, those obstacles initially present themselves as distractions. This is why this activity is so important to the conversation about grit.

EXTRINSIC MOTIVATION

TIMES I HAVE ACTED BECAUSE OF A REWARD

EXTRINSIC REWARDS I HAVE BEEN GIVEN

Extrinsic Motivation

Extrinsic motivation is when we do something we do not want to do because we will be given a reward (Deci, Koestner, & Ryan, 2001). Rewards include grades, prizes, praise from parents, money, and so on. We want students to understand what motivates them, which is an activity that we usually do not spend time on with young people. However, we should, so let's do it!

Ask students to fill in the boxes on this page. In the top box, they will describe specific things they did because they knew they would get a reward. In the bottom, they will list the different rewards they have been given. This is another opportunity for students to share in pairs, small groups, or whole class, as hearing someone else's story may trigger memories for them.

INTRINSIC MOTIVATION

THINGS I HAVE DONE BECAUSE I ENJOY THEM

HOW IT FEELS TO BE INTRINSICALLY MOTIVATED

Laila Y. Sanguras 2022, *Ready-to-Use Resources for Grit in the Classroom*, Routledge

Intrinsic Motivation

Intrinsic motivation is the opposite of extrinsic motivation. It is when we do something because it is satisfying – the reward comes from inside, not from something we are given (Deci, Koestner, & Ryan, 2001).

Model your responses to the prompts and then have students write their responses. In the top box, they will list the things they have done for no other reason than they enjoy them. In the bottom box, they need to articulate how that feels. For example, I have run at least one mile every day for over three years. No one pays me, sadly, and I do it without expectation of any external rewards. However, I like the way it feels after I finish a run and I find it satisfying to periodically add up the days in my run streak. Once students have generated their responses, provide an opportunity for them to share with one another.

FAILURE ⛓ SELF-WORTH

I was unsuccessful this year when I . . .	From this experience, I learned . . .	To be more successful next time, I will . . .
1.		
2.		
3.		

Laila Y. Sanguras 2022, *Ready-to-Use Resources for Grit in the Classroom*, Routledge

Failure ≠ Self-Worth

This activity is an important one and the graphic at the top explicitly depicts what we need to do: Break the chain that connects our idea of who we are (our value and self-worth) to our failures and accomplishments. Remind students that they are going to inevitably fail or fall short of their goals when they are striving for great things. This is normal and is not at all related to their self-worth. What IS related to self-worth, however, is how we respond to that failure.

In the first column, have students write three things they did this year that was unsuccessful. You may want to model this or provide ideas. Remind them that this does not have to be something huge like failing a class — it can be that low grade on a test or hurting a friend's feelings or not scoring at their soccer game. In the middle column, they need to write down something they learned from each experience. (Remind them about the difference between productive and unproductive failures.) Then in the last column, have them describe a plan for how they can do better next time. Encourage them to be as specific as possible.

Chapter 5: Poised for Success

Remember earlier that I told you that you are a Hope Dealer – and you absolutely are! But you also have the responsibility to help students build that internal hope, gratitude, and optimism that will get them through difficult times. We know that the world can be a scary, awful place and we want students armed with all of the tools they need to navigate their futures successfully. They can do this and you can help them!

Optimism is an important trait in gritty people (Duckworth & Eskreis-Winkler, 2013). In this chapter, students will be asked to practice gratitude as a way to build that sense of optimism. There are eight activities included in this chapter:

1. Gratitudes
2. Act Like a Winner
3. Practice Optimism
4. Attitude of Gratitude
5. You Are the Captain
6. I Need …
7. I've Learned about Myself
8. Thank You

DOI: 10.4324/9781003237617-7

I HAVE AN ATTITUDE OF GRATITUDE

FIVE GRATITUDES FOR TODAY...

Laila Y. Sanguras 2022, *Ready-to-Use Resources for Grit in the Classroom*, Routledge

Gratitudes

Maya Angelou (2013), a poet and civil rights activist, tweeted, "This is a wonderful day. I've never seen this one before." Take some time to talk through Angelou's quote and what it means, particularly focusing on the fact that there is something wonderful we can learn every day (even on our worst days). Then explain that researchers have found that there is a positive relationship between practicing gratitude and happiness (Witvliet et al., 2019) – this means that when one variable increases, the other variable increases. There is also a negative relationship between gratitude and depression and anxiety (Petrocchi, & Couyoumdjian, 2016) which means that when we regularly practice gratitude, we are less likely to feel sad and anxious thoughts. This is huge, y'all!

In this activity, have students write down five things for which they are grateful. The trick, though, is that they need to be specific. Instead of just writing that they are thankful for their family, they can write something like they are grateful to their moms for making their lunches every day. Or that they are thankful that their dads try to make them laugh when they are feeling sad. I want to encourage you to regularly practice this with students. Gratitude is not a "one and done" activity; it is something that should be practiced repeatedly so that appreciation and thankfulness become habits.

ACT *THE WAY YOU WANT TO* FEEL

- GRETCHEN RUBIN

Act Like a Winner

Gretchen Rubin (2009), an author and speaker, wrote that we should "Act the way you want to feel." Talk through what this means with students. There is research to suggest that if you want to feel a certain way (happy, confident, etc.), then you first need to start acting that way and THEN you will start to feel that way. Tell your students to try it sometime – it works!

Suggest that students look back at the feelings they wrote down in the "How does it feel to be the winner in your life" activity. In the corresponding trophy on this page, students should write down what each feeling looks like when they are acting that way. It is important that students are true to who they are. For example, if I wrote "excited" as one of my feelings, I would not write "jumping up and down" as my action because I am not that kind of person. My friend is, so she would write that. I would write that I would have a big smile on my face and laugh a lot.

WORDS I TELL MYSELF

1. _____

2. _____

3. _____

4. _____

5. _____

Laila Y. Sanguras 2022, *Ready-to-Use Resources for Grit in the Classroom*, Routledge

Practice Optimism

Remember when we talked about how we need to be optimistic if we want to have a growth mindset and be gritty? We need to practice that first.

In this activity, have students write down five things they tell themselves in their heads to be optimistic. (Give them some examples: Do not give up. You can do this. You have done harder things before. You are a nice person and your friends love you.) From there, you could lead a class discussion. You could also give them a piece of paper, have them write an optimistic statement on it without their names, and then hang the papers up in the room or around the school. Just like we want gratitude to become a habit, we also want optimism to be completely ingrained in who we are. And remember, this is important for you as well! You cannot be a Hope Dealer if you are not optimistic, so take some time to practice.

FIVE GRATITUDES FOR TODAY...

Laila Y. Sanguras 2022, *Ready-to-Use Resources for Grit in the Classroom*, Routledge

Attitude of Gratitude

In an earlier activity, I discussed the importance of gratitude and the relationship between gratitude and happiness (Witvliet et al., 2019). I also explained the powerful relationship between gratitude and happiness, which is why it is important that we regularly practice being appreciative.

In this activity, have students write down five things for which they are thankful. Remind them to be specific and provide examples of what not to do and what to do. For example, a non-example is "I am thankful for my dog" and an example is "I am thankful that my dog is so excited when I come home that she jumps up to kiss my face every time, whether I've been gone for 5 days or 5 minutes."

YOU ARE THE
CAPTAIN
WHO IS ON YOUR TEAM?

PEOPLE WHO CHEER ME ON NO MATTER WHAT

PEOPLE WHO KNOW ME BETTER THAN ANYONE AND ALWAYS SUPPORT ME

PEOPLE WHO SET ME STRAIGHT WHEN I GET OFF TRACK

Laila Y. Sanguras 2022, *Ready-to-Use Resources for Grit in the Classroom*, Routledge

You Are the Captain

It is important to know who is on our team as we go through life. This activity is designed to help us think through our teams. At the top of the page, students will write down the names of people who will never give up on them no matter what. In the middle, they will write the names of the people who know their deepest and darkest secrets and they will always support them. (These can be the same people.) At the bottom of the page, they will write the names of people who will let them know when they are messing up and need to do better. There may be overlap, but there also may be people who fit into only one or two of the boxes. This might be tricky for students to conceptualize, so it would be helpful for you to brainstorm with students based on the people in your life. You could even do this activity based on characters in a story or a class novel that you have read.

IN ORDER TO BE GRITTY, I NEED MY

TEACHER TO KNOW/DO	FAMILY TO KNOW/DO

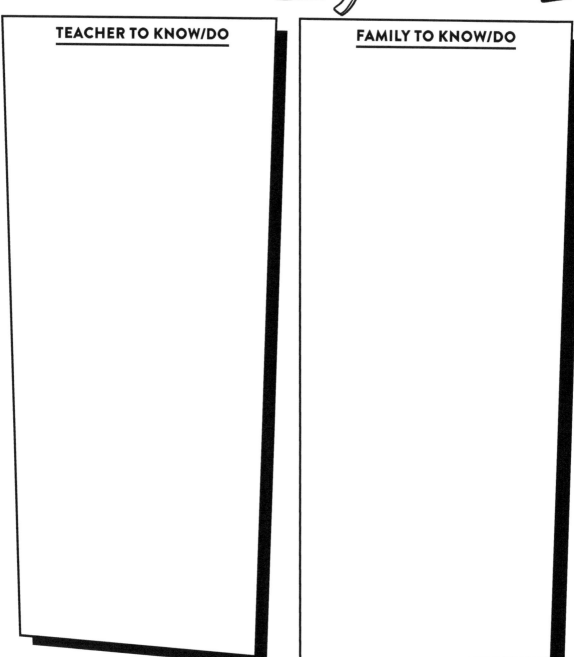

I Need ...

By now we know that grit means that we must pursue our interests regularly and that we need to be challenged (so that we can overcome those challenges). It is time think about how the people in our lives can support us in this pursuit.

I suggest that you model this for your students. Then, have them brainstorm what they need their future teacher to know/do to support their quest to be gritty. For example, they may want their future teachers to know that they need them to be patient when explaining a math problem. What about their family? For example, they may need their family to know that they want honest feedback about how they played at their soccer game, and not just the typical "good job." Ask students to share so that they can generate new ideas and add to their lists. The whole point of this activity is that students of all ages should have a concept of what they need from the people in their lives. This way they are more able to identify their helpers in times of need.

THIS YEAR, I've Learned About Myself...

1. _____

2. _____

3. _____

4. _____

5. _____

Laila Y. Sanguras 2022, *Ready-to-Use Resources for Grit in the Classroom*, Routledge

I've Learned About Myself

At the end of the year, remind students that this has been a fun and focused year on passion and perseverance. Ask students to identify five things they have learned about themselves. Give them time to go back through the activities they have completed to see how they have grown and changed. Maybe they learned that it feels good to show appreciation to the people in their lives or that they can improve their math grade if they really try or that they don't really like soccer as much as they thought they did. This is another great opportunity for students to share with the class or with small groups. Celebrate their growth!

THANK YOU

Who are five people for whom you are thankful and why are you thankful for them? Be specific.

Laila Y. Sanguras 2022, *Ready-to-Use Resources for Grit in the Classroom*, Routledge

Thank You

When we think about gratitude, it is also important to take the time to recognize the people for whom we are thankful. In this activity, ask students to write down the names of five people and why they are thankful for them. Remind them to be specific and encourage them to take this to the next step by writing a letter, calling, or even sending a text sharing their gratitude for each person. If you have time (and you want to work on those letter-writing skills or – GASP – how to address an actual envelope), you might build in a letter-writing activity into your lessons.

Chapter 6: Pursuing Passion

I cannot imagine anything scarier than sitting at my high school graduation ceremony and hearing a speaker announce, "Go. Find your passion." I am sure that I heard a version of those words many years ago and that they continue to be repeated every year. Every time I hear it, I want to scream, "BUT WHAT DOES THAT MEAN?" How can we expect an 18-year-old to all of a sudden find a passion? The answer is that we cannot. But what we can do is start building in time for students to think about and pursue different passions.

We have to be committed to this. We have too many kids who are directionless, so they go to college because they think that is what they are supposed to do (Hersh & Merrow, 2005). We have far too many college graduates with degrees and no plan of action (Carnevale, Hanson, & Gulish, 2013). We have too many young adults, "Boomerang Kids," moving back in to live with their parents because they just do not know what to do with their lives (Fry, 2016). Can you imagine anything scarier? (I mean, I am mainly talking about the kids here, but the parents must also be pretty freaked out. I realize that there are economical and social-emotional reasons why a child may move back home; I am not talking about those situations in this case.) So let's do something about the problem before it gets to freak-out level scary.

In this chapter, students will be asked to build upon their work in Chapter 3, "Cultivating Curiosity," to further explore the things about which they are passionate. Nine student activities are included:

1. Big 10 Challenge
2. Talent Brainstorm
3. Success in 20 Years
4. From Talent to Success
5. Road Map to Super Stretch Goal Success
6. My Favorites
7. Turning Skills into Achievements
8. Connecting Interests
9. Reporting My Research

DOI: 10.4324/9781003237617-8

BIG 10 CHALLENGE

TOPIC _____

1. _____

2. _____

3. _____

4. _____

5. _____

6. _____

7. _____

8. _____

9. _____

10. _____

Laila Y. Sanguras 2022, *Ready-to-Use Resources for Grit in the Classroom*, Routledge

Big 10 Challenge

Passion is an important component of grit (Duckworth, 2016), so it is important that students have a clear idea of their interests. In this activity, we are going to dig in deeper to an area of interest. Ask students to choose one topic they want to know more about – this can be something from their "I wonder" lists or related to the "Did you know" brainstorm. (Another option is that you can give a list of topics they will study during the year and have them choose one that sounds the most interesting. Choice is important here, so be sure to provide options.)

Give students time to research their topics and then they need to write down ten fun facts about their topics. Explain to them that the facts they write have to be interesting, deep dives into the topic. The goal of this is to have them skim past the facts that everyone knows about and really get to the heart of why this is an interesting topic. Encourage them to share.

SUCCESS and TALENT

ARE NOT THE SAME THING.
—RACHEL HOLLIS

Brainstorm all the talents you have.

Laila Y. Sanguras 2022, *Ready-to-Use Resources for Grit in the Classroom*, Routledge

Talent Brainstorm

Rachel Hollis (2019), an author and motivational speaker, said, "Dude, talent and success are not the same thing." Facilitate a conversation with your students on what it means to have a talent and what it means to be successful. Ask them what they think Rachel Hollis means by her quote. Ask for examples of people who were talented, but not successful. You can offer a personal story of a talent you have/had, but it did not lead anywhere successful. For example, maybe you had some talent as a soccer player when you were a child, but that did not mean that you went on to play for the U.S. women's soccer team. You had a talent, but that did not necessarily lead to you being successful in that area.

Ask students to brainstorm at least ten talents they have. Encourage them to think about things they can physically do (i.e., dance, sing, run fast, spell, cook, put together creative outfits, etc.) as well as things related to psychosocial skills (i.e., making people laugh, cheering up their friends, noticing when someone needs a friend, etc.). Share your own list as well. You can find a place to display these in your classroom.

IMAGINE YOURSELF IN 20 YEARS...

Someone describes you as being successful. What does that look like?

Laila Y. Sanguras 2022, *Ready-to-Use Resources for Grit in the Classroom*, Routledge

Success in 20 Years

Part of my conception of grit is it is important to identify obstacles so that we can plan our way around or through them. It is also important to dream, set Super Stretch Goals, and to have a clear idea of what it means to be successful.

In this activity, tell students to imagine that they overheard a parent/friend/teacher talking about them in 20 years. In the space provided, have them write down what that person says about them. (The purpose of this activity is for them to define what success looks like to them, so you want to be careful not to define it for them. For example, some may think having a big house is how they imagine their success. Others might think it means that they have traveled to every continent. Or they are a famous actor. Or they have a spouse and children. Or they have graduated from college. You get the idea … Help them without imposing your ideas about success on them.)

List 3 talents you have.

Describe how you can use your talents to be successful.

Laila Y. Sanguras 2022, *Ready-to-Use Resources for Grit in the Classroom*, Routledge

From Talent to Success

To begin this activity, ask students to revisit their Talent Brainstorms and choose three talents from their lists. From there, they will list those three talents on the left side of the page. On the right side of the page, ask them to define what it means to be successful in that talent. For example, if a talent is that they are good at basketball, success could mean that they play in the NBA or make the high school basketball team or become a basketball coach, and so on. Again, the point is to create personal definitions of what success looks like for each talent.

Road Map to Super Stretch Goal Success

Begin this activity by brainstorming a conversation about obstacles. To do this, share a personal or academic/professional goal (maybe your own or make one up). Then brainstorm all of the things that might get in the way of someone accomplishing that goal. Then have students imagine the ways they can handle those obstacles. For example, if an obstacle is not having enough time, maybe a solution is to cut out some time from playing video games.

Next, ask students to write their Academic Super Stretch Goal at the top of the page. Inside each road sign, they should write an obstacle that could get in the way of achieving the SSG. Inside the road (next to each sign), have them write down how they can handle that obstacle. Remind them to be as specific as possible.

MY FAVORITE SUBJECTS

MY FAVORITE THINGS TO DO ON THE WEEKENDS

MY FAVORITE BOOKS

MY FAVORITE MOVIES

MY FAVORITE . . .

Laila Y. Sanguras 2022, *Ready-to-Use Resources for Grit in the Classroom*, Routledge

My Favorites

Remind students that having a passion (or several) is important to being gritty, and that passion stems from things we enjoy doing (and are good at). To explore our interests, this activity is designed to help students identify their favorite things.

Give students time to brainstorm responses in each box. For the bottom box, students can pick any category they want – you can help them brainstorm potential categories (favorite musicians, video games, gifts they have received, athletic activities, crafts, etc.). Once they are done brainstorming their favorites, have them connect with a partner to share one category AND why they listed those things in that category. (The point of this is for them to identify what they like, but then why they like these things. Knowing that can help steer them in the direction of identifying interests and passions.)

HOW CAN I TURN MY SKILLS INTO ACHIEVEMENTS

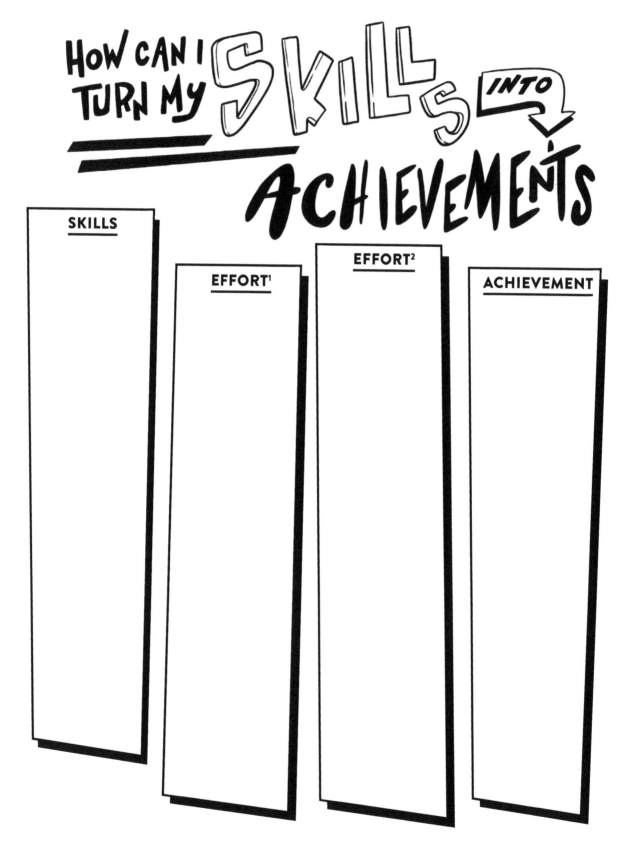

SKILLS

EFFORT[1]

EFFORT[2]

ACHIEVEMENT

Laila Y. Sanguras 2022, *Ready-to-Use Resources for Grit in the Classroom*, Routledge

Turning Skills into Achievements

Remind students of the equation Skill x Effort^2 = Achievement and that Effort counts twice (Duckworth, 2016)! This activity is an opportunity to put this equation into action.

In the first column, tell students to list three to five skills they have. In the next column, they will write down an effort (something they can do) to turn that skill into a talent. In the next column, they will write down another thing they can do to turn that skill into an achievement. (See what we are doing here? Doubling up the effort to increase the likelihood of achieving in that area!) In the last column, students should identify what the achievement is that could be the result of each skill, effort, and talent.

YOUR INTERESTS ARE NOT RANDOM

LET'S CONNECT THEM.

Laila Y. Sanguras 2022, *Ready-to-Use Resources for Grit in the Classroom*, Routledge

Connecting Interests

If we believe that curiosity leads to interest which leads to passion (and we do believe that!), we need to help students think about their interests and how they all might be related. These can be hobbies they have, things they like to do in school, types of music they like, and so on.

In each of the raindrops, tell students write down an interest they have. Then in the umbrella, have them write down how all of the interests are connected. You can model your interest connections for them. An example might be that their interests are baking cookies, playing cards, shooting hoops, rap music, and football. A connection could be that these are all things they do with other people, they don't involve much reading/writing, and so on. (I basically described my son.)

REPORTING MY RESEARCH

Reporting My Research

In our pursuit of identifying passions and cultivating curiosity, this year has hopefully been full of opportunities for students to research different interests. Encourage students to look back at their "I Used to Wonder" and "Inquiring Minds" pages and choose one topic.

From there, have students come up with a creative, intriguing title that will make other students want to know more about this. For example, maybe they used to wonder what kind of waterproof mascara is the best so they researched and found out that Revlon lasts the longest and Maybelline is the worst. So they create a catchy title like "Heartbroken Girls Swear Off Boys and Maybelline Forever." (After reading this, you want to know more, right? That's the point! We want all students to be curious! By the way, I have no idea which waterproof mascara is the best, so please don't come for me.)

Students will write their titles inside the frame. But to take this to the next level, have students recreate this frame on a piece of paper and display it around the classroom or school. At the bottom, they can add a disclaimer like "For more information, see Joe [or whatever their name is]." I can just picture all of the students scrambling up to Joe asking for the details!

Chapter 7: Profiles of Gritty People

I love learning people's stories. I appreciate people who are vulnerable and open to talking about their struggles; in fact, vulnerability is one of my favorite qualities in a person and I believe it is the key to deep connection. I appreciate it so much because I see myself in other people's struggles. I mean, sure, I am not J.Lo who had a very public breakup with baseball superstar Alex Rodriguez, but I have had messy breakups that felt humiliating and incredibly painful. While I do not know the details of their story, I know what I saw: I saw a woman committed to taking care of her children, improving her health, and finding happiness. While she has a life that is drastically different from mine, I can learn from her roadmap.

In this chapter, I share stories of gritty people with prompts for discussion and reflection. I have included 11 profiles of diverse individuals that I hope your students will find interesting:

1. Steve Chen, YouTube founder
2. Patricia Medici, conservation biologist
3. Cordelia Cranshaw, Miss District of Columbia 2019
4. Jennifer Lashbrook, artist
5. Kid President, motivational speaker
6. Jason Lester, athlete
7. Ariana Grande, singer and actress
8. Gunner Gillett, aspiring sports announcer
9. Sucheta Kripalani, politician
10. Benjamin "Kickz" Kapelushnik, social media influencer and entrepreneur
11. You Choose!

DOI: 10.4324/9781003237617-9

STEVE CHEN

How do you imagine Chen felt growing up?
Have you ever felt this way?

Laila Y. Sanguras 2022, *Ready-to-Use Resources for Grit in the Classroom*, Routledge

Steve Chen

Steve Chen was one of the founders of YouTube (oh how I wish I had been a part of that group …). As you tell his story, I suggest that you show students his picture as well. Chen was born in Taiwan and moved to the United States when he was eight years old (Biography.com Editors, 2021). He lived his life as a Taiwanese boy at home – speaking Taiwanese and living within the Taiwanese culture – and as an American boy at school – speaking English and trying to fit in with his American peers. Math was always easy for him until he transferred schools to the Illinois Mathematics and Science Academy in 10th grade. When he was there, he realized that he was not the smartest kid in the class anymore, which really challenged his belief about himself. While attending school, he also worked at 7–11 and a local grocery store (Steve Chen, 2021).

In this activity, have students write down how they think Chen felt growing up, living a double life. Did this cause him any challenges? How do they think Chen felt when he went from being at the top of the class at one school to not at another school? What about how Chen may have felt trying to balance school and his personal life with work?

Patrícia Medici

What are the unique challenges Medici faces while trying to protect tapirs?

Laila Y. Sanguras 2022, *Ready-to-Use Resources for Grit in the Classroom*, Routledge

Patricia Medici

As you tell the story of Patricia Medici (n.d.), show students her picture (preferably one with tapirs in it). You can also show this short video on the tapir: www.youtube.com/watch?v=PFRrsX_HxD8. Medici is from Brazil and knew she wanted to study the tapir, the largest land mammal in South America, right after college. Tapirs can be difficult to study because they are solitary and nocturnal. They are currently being threatened by poachers, the ruin of their habitats, and can become roadkill (Medici, 2015). She started an organization called the Lowland Tapir Conservation Initiative (LTCI) solely focused on saving the tapir and she won the Future for Nature Award, which gave the LTCI money to continue their efforts. Her team installed cameras throughout the woods in Brazil so that they could learn more about tapirs' behaviors. They also attached GPS enabled reflective collars to tapirs so that they can be easily tracked and seen at night when crossing highways. Medici says that she plans to work on the conservation of tapirs for the rest of her life.

In groups or individually, have students brainstorm and list all of the challenges that Medici has faced throughout her career. This would be a great time for you to jigsaw the conversation. An example of a jigsaw is when you put four students in a group and name them A, B, C, and D. Give them time to brainstorm responses to the question. Then have all of the As meet together, the Bs meet together, and so on. They can share their ideas and add to their lists. Remember that the point is to remind students that everyone faces challenges, but that it is how we deal with those challenges that determine our success.

CORDELIA CRANSHAW

What were the pivotal moments in Cordelia Cranshaw's life when she could have given up, but instead pushed herself forward? Why do you think she didn't give up?

Laila Y. Sanguras 2022, *Ready-to-Use Resources for Grit in the Classroom*, Routledge

Cordelia Cranshaw

In this activity, you will tell students the story of Cordelia Cranshaw, Miss D.C. 2019 (you might want to show her picture as well). Her mom was sentenced to prison and her dad was an alcoholic, so she was put into foster care at 14 years old (Who is Cordelia Cranshaw? n.d.). She grew up in foster care, moving around from home to home. She was told throughout her life that she would never amount to anything, that she would get pregnant at an early age, and end up homeless or in jail. She knew she did not want this to be her story, so she graduated from high school, went to college, and earned her Masters degree in social work. She realized early on that education was the key to living the life she wanted. She also started an organization called Acts of Random Kindness (ARK) that supports children with incarcerated parents and families who live in poverty.

When she was a teenager, Cranshaw entered her first beauty pageant because she saw it as a pathway out of the life she was living. She competed for the 2016 title of Miss D.C. and did not place out of the 16 other women in the pageant. She tried twice more, in 2017 and 2018, and placed fourth. Then she won in 2019. She currently works to empower young people who live in situations like hers, explaining that their circumstances need to be their motivation for living better lives. She explains that this starts by loving yourself and then setting goals and working harder than anyone else to achieve them.

Once you have shared Cranshaw's story, ask students to respond to the prompts: What were the pivotal moments in Cordelia Cranshaw's life when she could have given up, but instead pushed herself forward? Why do you think she did not give up? You can also ask students how they may have responded if they found themselves in similar situations.

JENNIFER LASHBROOK

What can you learn from Lashbrook about pursuing your interests?

Laila Y. Sanguras 2022, *Ready-to-Use Resources for Grit in the Classroom*, Routledge

Jennifer Lashbrook

Jennifer Lashbrook is an artist – you may want to pull up a picture of her and her work. (Select a work of art from this page and then also pull up the actual work so that students can see how they compare. Link to website: www.jenniferlashbrook.com/.) Lashbrook says that she has always been obsessed with color, which set her on the path to break down images by using pixilated color swatches (like the paint swatches you find at a paint store; About, n.d.). She likes taking existing works of art (portraits and landscapes) and recreating them using this pixilated technique. When viewed up close, you see the swatches of color. When viewed from far away or through a camera on a phone, the image becomes clearer.

Lashbrook has had her work displayed on two television shows (*Empire* and *Beats*) and has been written up in many publications (including *Forbes*). She also has work displayed in Hilton hotels, participates in shows around the country, and has won many awards. Her love for art began when she was ten and took an oil painting class one summer. She studied art in high school and college, exploring different mediums (making jewelry, drawing, etc.). She thinks of her current style of art as the adult version of a puzzle (Meet Jennifer Lashbrook, 2019).

Have students respond to the prompt on the page: What can you learn from Lashbrook about pursuing your interests? Ask them to think about Lashbrook's creativity in moving from traditional painting to using color swatches to create art. How can they be creative in the pursuit of the things they are interested in? What can they learn from her story that applies to their own?

Kid President

Why do you think Kid President is popular? What do you admire about him?

Kid President

Kid President's real name is Robby Novak. (A playlist of his videos can be found here – select one to play for your class: www.youtube.com/playlist?list=PLzvRx_johoA-YabI6FWcU-jL6nKA1Um-t.) Novak has a disease called osteogenesis imperfecta, which can cause his bones to be very brittle and break easily. He has steel rods in both legs, has broken over 90 bones, and has had 15 surgeries, but most people would not know this just by his social media presence (Hammitt, 2019). He and his younger sister, who also has the disease, were adopted when they were young.

Novak and his brother-in-law started creating the Kid President videos for the family, but they soon became an internet sensation (Editors, TheFamousPeople.com, n.d.). His videos have been viewed over 100 million times, he's met Beyoncé, President Obama, and his book *Kid President's Guide to Being Awesome* was on the New York Times bestseller list for five weeks. His mission is to make the world a better place by spreading joy (Hammitt, 2019).

In this activity, have students respond to the prompt: Why do you think Kid President is popular? What do you admire about him? Ask students to share their responses to open up a conversation about the character traits and qualities that may have led to Novak's success.

JASON —— —
— — — LESTER

Which of Lester's accomplishments is most impressive to you? What lesson can you learn about overcoming obstacles from Lester's story?

Laila Y. Sanguras 2022, *Ready-to-Use Resources for Grit in the Classroom*, Routledge

Jason Lester

When Jason Lester was 12 years old, he lived with his dad and loved playing football and baseball. While riding his bike one day, he was hit by a woman who was driving 70 miles per hour and was left to die on the side of the road. He had 21 broken bones and a collapsed lung. His right arm was paralyzed as a result of the hit-and-run accident, yet he continued to play sports. Additionally, while he was recovering in the hospital, his father died (Jason P. Lester, 2021).

When Lester turned 18, he was the #2 ranked biathlon competitor in Arizona. (A biathlon is a combination of rifle shooting and cross-country skiing. It really is an amazing sport that I never knew existed until today.) As an adult, he began to compete in Ironman and Ultraman competitions. In 2007 he was named a PC Athlete of the Year finalist by USA Triathlon and founded the Never Stop Foundation where athletes work with kids to build resilience and confidence. In 2009, he won an ESPY award for Best Male Athlete with a Disability. In 2012, he ran 26 marathons in 26 consecutive days. In 2013, he ran 3,500 miles across the United States in 72 days to raise money for Hurricane Sandy victims. In 2014, he became the first person to run the Great Wall of China in a single attempt – it is 2,500 miles long and took him 85 days. He also wrote a book called *Running on Faith* (Jason P. Lester, 2021).

Wow! That is quite a list of accomplishments! In this reflection, ask students to consider which of Lester's accomplishments they find most impressive. Additionally, ask students to identify any lessons they can learn about overcoming obstacles from Lester's amazing story. I suggest that you also provide students an opportunity to discuss their responses with a partner or with the class.

ARIANA GRANDE

What are some of the personal and professional struggles that Ariana Grande has overcome? What have you experienced that was similar?

Laila Y. Sanguras 2022, *Ready-to-Use Resources for Grit in the Classroom*, Routledge

Ariana Grande

Ariana Grande grew up in Florida. When she was in elementary school, her parents divorced and she regularly met with a counselor to help her with her feelings about the divorce. She loved acting and singing – the first time she was on television was when she sang the "Star-Spangled Banner" at a Florida Panthers hockey game when she was eight years old. (Here is the video: www.youtube.com/watch?v=QEwwhkIDbVo) At the age of ten, she co-founded Kids Who Care, a youth singing group that performed at charity events (Bustillo, n.d.). They helped raise over $500,000. She became famous as an actress when she starred on the Nickelodeon show *Victorious*, and later on the spinoff *Sam & Cat* (Ariana Grande, 2021).

When she was 13, Grande told her managers that she wanted to transition from acting to singing (and that she wanted to sing R&B). Her managers told her no one would buy an R&B album from someone so young. She continued to act, but also sang covers of different artists (Mariah Carey, Adele, and Whitney Houston) and uploaded them to YouTube. Her music career took off and she eventually became the first solo artist to place in the top three spots on the Billboard Hot 100 music chart (Ariana Grande, 2021).

In 2017, Grande was on tour in Manchester, England, when a suicide bomber detonated a bomb after her concert. She was openly devastated (23 people were killed and over 500 people were injured) and canceled the rest of her tour. She then recruited artists (Justin Bieber, Miley Cyrus, etc.) and gave a televised benefit concert that raised $23 million to benefit the victims and their families. In 2017, Billboard named her Female Artist of the Year. She was also sued over an image that appeared in one of her music videos, but the lawsuit was dropped (Associated Press, 2019). In 2018, her former boyfriend died of a drug overdose, which devastated her. She adopted his dog (and now has at least ten dogs, one of which is named Snape after the Harry Potter character). In 2019, she was the youngest and only the fourth female to headline the Coachella Valley Music and Arts Festival. She has been nominated for six Grammy Awards, won three American Music Awards, and two MTV Music Awards. She has also launched seven different fragrances ("Ariana Grande," 2021).

Quite a life, right? We want students to understand that famous people encounter setbacks and challenges just like us. Ask students to respond to the prompts: What are some of the personal and professional struggles that Ariana Grande has overcome? What have you experienced that was similar? If time, allow students to discuss with the class or in small groups.

GUNNER GILLETT

What do you think about Gillett's belief about losing?

HEADSNAPS & HEAD GEAR

Laila Y. Sanguras 2022, *Ready-to-Use Resources for Grit in the Classroom*, Routledge

Gunner Gillett

Gunner Gillett is a 14-year-old athlete and YouTuber with a channel called Headsnaps and Head Gear. He started as a sports announcer when he was six and would announce at the baseball games his dad coached. He loved it! He realized he was passionate about competition and loved public speaking, so he worked with his parents to figure out what he could do. He decided he wanted to interview wrestlers and wrestling coaches, and then share his interviews with others. His mom taught him how to edit the videos and she is usually the one who films the interviews.

Even though he loves sports, Gillett was not born with the ideal physical attributes – he is not huge compared to other athletes his age and has had issues with his lungs and legs. But he put that behind him and just tried to be better than his opponents. He has run into issues at times since he is young and has not been taken seriously as an interviewer, but he continues to work on improving his skills by practicing and attending broadcasting camps. Gillett says that when you fail or do not succeed, it is because of one of two things: 1) you didn't practice hard enough or 2) you're not good enough. He says you do not want to be the person who fails because you did not work hard enough.

This journal prompt could really spark some interesting discussions. Ask students to write down whether they agree or disagree with Gillett's belief about losing and then open up the debate to a larger class discussion. Ask students for evidence to support or refute his claim as a way to really consider what he meant about losing.

SUCHETA KRIPALANI

What can you learn from Kripalani about pursuing your goals?

Sucheta Kripalani

Sucheta Kripalani was the first female Chief Minister of the largest Indian province and served as the head of the government for four years. She grew up being very self-conscious about her looks and never felt very smart. Her father's job caused them to move quite a bit as well. When she was ten, she overheard her father talking to friends about the Jallianwala Bagh massacre, a time when British troops fired into a crowd of people and killed many. Kripalani says that this was the start of her beliefs about India establishing its independence from Britain (Sucheta Kripalani, 2021).

As an adult, Kripalani met Ghandi and joined the Indian National Congress. She believed in the principles of Ghandi's movement and adhered to them throughout her career (Baldwa, 2020). Once she retired from politics, she and her husband donated all their money and resources to an organization that assisted disadvantaged people living in the capital.

Ask students what they can learn from Kripalani about pursuing their goals. They can write a reflection and then share in a small group.

BENJAMIN KICKZ KAPELUSHNIK

If you follow the advice of Kapelushnik's mom, what would you be doing right now?

Laila Y. Sanguras 2022, *Ready-to-Use Resources for Grit in the Classroom*, Routledge

Benjamin "Kickz" Kapelushnik

Benjamin Kapelushnik is a teenage social media influencer and entrepreneur. His parents are Russian immigrants and he grew up in Florida. He sells hard-to-find sneakers to people willing to pay top dollar. His love for shoes began in middle school when his mom bought him a pair of Nikes and he received a lot of positive attention for them. He started using all his money on sneakers and even attended sneaker conventions. (Who even knew these were a thing???) He began to explore what it would take to resell his sneakers (Benjamin Kapelushnik, 2021).

In seventh grade, Kapelushnik started to campout at stores to buy highly popular sneakers before they sold out. When he was in eighth grade, he bought a pair of Lebron X MVPs for $400 and resold them for $4,000. He turned that into more sneakers that he could buy and resell. He then sold some of his sneakers to DJ Khaled who asked him how business was going. Kapelushnik responded, "Boomin'" which became the catch phrase for his company (Ocbazghi, 2018). He says his biggest customer is P. Diddy, who buys sneakers in bulk and that he has made over $1 million dollars so far and plans to go to college to study business. He also says that his mom gave him the best advice he has ever received: Follow your dream and your passion (Marinova, 2016).

In this reflection, ask students to describe what they would be doing right in this moment if they were following the advice of Kapelushnik's mom. What would it look like if they were actively pursuing their dreams and passions? This could also lead to a great discussion about how their descriptions may have been different several years ago or how they may look different five years down the road.

Who is a person you admire?

Laila Y. Sanguras 2022, *Ready-to-Use Resources for Grit in the Classroom*, Routledge

You Choose!

I have provided you with profiles of several gritty people, but we know that we want students invested in this idea that success and struggle are a package. This means that they need to identify the people they admire so now it is time for them to choose someone. Remind them that they do not need to know the person's story – anyone who has ever accomplished something great has had an intense interest in that thing AND has had to overcome obstacles along the way. So they just pick someone they want to study and do some investigating.

In this activity, students can fill in the box with the person's name; they can also draw a picture of him/ her if they want. Then they need to research the person and write down some examples of what makes them gritty.

GRIT IN THE CLASSROOM

Chapter 8: What Do I Stand For?

I included this final chapter because I believe we have an awesome responsibility of helping our students find themselves. We spend an incredible amount of time with them, which can be exhausting for sure. But it is also exhilarating. We have the opportunity to help them understand who they are. Sure, we want them to be gritty, but we also want them to think about how they can improve the world around them. We want them to know that they are amazing, unique, and fascinating – and that there is no one in the world exactly like them. That is powerful stuff.

We want students to have a sense of who they are and what matters to them. This chapter is designed to have students articulate what drives them. I provide you with seven activities focused on this:

1. Why Does Grit Matter?
2. Values
3. Problem Finding
4. How I Want to Live My Life
5. Not a Pretzel
6. What Do I Stand For?
7. Turning Beliefs into Action

DOI: 10.4324/9781003237617-10

WHY DOES GRIT MATTER?

HAPPINESS

PERFORMANCE

METACOGNITION

Why Does Grit Matter?

It is important that students understand why grit matters, especially if we are committed to weaving grit-building activities throughout our lessons all year. First, talk through what the words on this activity page mean (happiness, performance, and metacognition) so that we are all operating with shared definitions.

Then, share the research on each of these topics and how they relate to grit. As you are sharing, instruct your students to take notes on each topic to help him/her remember why grit matters.

Happiness: Grit, positive affect, happiness, and life satisfaction are significantly positively correlated (Singh & Jha, 2008).

Performance: Grit is just an important an influence on success as cognitive ability (Duckworth, 2016). Researchers found that eighth-graders with higher self-discipline earned higher grades, achievement scores, and were more frequently admitted to an academically competitive high school (Duckworth & Seligman, 2005).

Metacognition: Perseverance is a consistent and adaptive predictor for all indicators of metacognition, motivation, and procrastination (Wolters & Hussain, 2015). Eighth-graders with higher self-discipline had better attendance and reported better study habits than their undisciplined peers (Duckworth & Seligman, 2005).

A VALUE IS A PRINCIPLE OF WHAT I BELIEVE IS IMPORTANT.

MY VALUES

WHAT DO I DO THAT SHOWS PEOPLE THESE ARE MY VALUES?

Laila Y. Sanguras 2022, *Ready-to-Use Resources for Grit in the Classroom*, Routledge

Values

"A value is a principle of what I believe is important." Talk through this statement with your students. Explain that our values are also our principles – they are what we stand for. You can also offer up some ideas of values: kindness, generosity, religious beliefs, hard work, and so on.

In the top box of the activity page, ask students to write down their values. Have them answer the questions "What do I value?" and "What is important to me?" In the bottom box, have them write down what they do to show people that these are their values. For example, if they say they value honesty, how do they show others that this is a principle that is important to them? They should write down how they manifest each value from the top box in the bottom box. You may need to model this for your students and, like I have done so many times before, I encourage you to provide time for students to share their responses.

STAY CURIOUS

Let's brainstorm all of the issues or problems you can imagine. Remember the essential rules of brainstorming: There are no bad ideas and don't overthink it.

ISSUES AROUND ME

ISSUES IN MY COMMUNITY

ISSUES IN THE WORLD

Laila Y. Sanguras 2022, *Ready-to-Use Resources for Grit in the Classroom*, Routledge

Problem Finding

In the previous chapter, I provided profiles of many gritty people who all noticed problems and then worked to fix/improve the situation. For example, Chen and his friends founded YouTube as a solution to a problem. There are several versions of the exact problem they were trying to solve. These include that 1) they were at a dinner party one night and took a bunch of videos, but didn't have a way to share them with each other (YouTube, 2021), 2) they wanted to create an online video dating website (Dredge, 2016), and 3) they realized it was difficult to find video clips of world events easily online (Rathi & Mishra, 2021). The truth doesn't actually matter here. What is important is the fact that Chen and his partners were curious about how to solve a problem. It has led them to pursue additional interests in technology that exceed YouTube – and it all started by curiosity. So, we are going to get curious.

Provide students with time to brainstorm problems that they think need to be solved – big problems, little problems, and so on. In the top box, students need to think about issues at home or at school. These can include problems with recycling, school lunch, school uniforms, trying to communicate with parents, siblings taking their stuff, for example. Then students need to brainstorm issues in their communities. These might include traffic, no sidewalks, littering, no Chinese food restaurants in town, slow internet, and so on. Finally, students will brainstorm issues in the world. These can be related to air pollution, human trafficking, national security, for example. Remind students of the rules of brainstorming: There are no bad ideas and do not overthink.

GROWTH

experiences

CONTRIBUTION

Laila Y. Sanguras 2022, *Ready-to-Use Resources for Grit in the Classroom*, Routledge

How I Want to Live My Life

One way to think about our futures is to think about our lives in three buckets:

- The first bucket is growth – what do we want to learn? What skills do we want to have? Is there a character trait we want to develop? What do we want to improve about ourselves?
- The second bucket is experiences – what do we want to do? What do we want to accomplish? What places do we want to explore?
- The third bucket is contribution – how do we want to contribute to the world? What kind of difference do we want to make in the lives of our friends and family? What will our legacies be?

We want students to have an idea of how they want to live their lives and what is important to them. Give students time to fill in each bucket on the page.

YOU ARE NOT A PRETZEL

—KAREN SALMANSOHN

15 WAYS TO DESCRIBE MYSELF

Laila Y. Sanguras 2022, *Ready-to-Use Resources for Grit in the Classroom*, Routledge

Not a Pretzel

Karen Salmansohn (2016) is an author who wants us to know that, "You are not a pretzel." (It is possible you are wondering where I'm headed with this, but please stick with me.) Tell students to imagine a pretzel – it starts as a piece of dough that can be shaped into anything! Then ask them what they think Salmonsohn means by her statement (hint: it is that they need to be true to who they are and not let people bend and twist them around).

In this activity, ask students to write down 15 ways that they would describe themselves. These can be just words (painter, shy) or phrases (loves to be challenged, Boy Scout). We want them to have an idea of who they are and we want them to have practiced articulating who they are. This ability will firm up their sense of self so that they are not easily "pretzeled."

WHAT DO I STAND FOR?

What Do I Stand For?

Earlier in our study of grit, we explored our values and principles and now we are going to revisit those. Ask students to write down the specific things that they stand for. Have them think about issues they have learned about in history or in the news. They can then identify what it is that they care so much about that they would stand up to someone about it. They will write these down. Encourage them to share with their partners or with the class. We want them to see the connectedness among their values, principles, and what they stand for. (The band fun. has a great song called "Some Nights" that asks "What do I stand for?" that you might consider playing for students (Bhasker et al., 2012). Be sure to look for the clean version and preview it ahead of time to verify the language and content are appropriate for your students.)

TURNING BELIEFS INTO ACTION

What actions can I take to show the world what I stand for?

1. _____

2. _____

3. _____

4. _____

5. _____

Laila Y. Sanguras 2022, *Ready-to-Use Resources for Grit in the Classroom*, Routledge

Turning Beliefs into Action

In the "What Do I Stand For" activity, students connected their values, principles, and what they stand for. This activity builds upon that one. We want students to now consider how they can show the world that this is important to them.

I suggest that you model this for students and give them examples. For example, if they wrote that they stand for equality, have them write down five specific actions they can take or decisions they can make to show everyone around them that equality is important to them. This list can then be a great starting point for a personal essay, connection to historical figures, and so on. As always, I encourage you to ask students to share their responses.

Quotes to Use for Bulletin Boards, Websites, and So On

In this section, I provide you with 12 quotes. You can post these on bulletin boards, your website, or anywhere you think they can be viewed by students and parents. There is also a final activity in this chapter where students can curate personalized lists of quotes, song lyrics, and images that they find motivating.

1. Grit is a mash-up of passion and perseverance.
2. Grit is just as important to my success as how smart I am.
3. Exposure to new ideas breeds new ideas.
4. Curiosity → Interest → Passion.
5. The most powerful voice I hear is my own.
6. Perseverance is a choice to keep pushing forward even when I want to give up.
7. Talent x Effort^2 = Achievement.
8. Hard work is a habit.
9. Passion creates movement.
10. It's crucial that I know my "why."
11. I'm either winning or I'm learning.
12. I can do hard things.

Talk through the statement: Grit is a mash-up of passion and perseverance. A mash-up is the combination of separate elements to create something new; that "something new" cannot exist without each of the different elements. It is a term often used in music. You can introduce the concept to your students by playing a mash-up of songs for them – you can choose specific artists or play a mash-up of the best songs of a certain year. (Be sure to preview these before sharing with your class to make sure they are appropriate.) Your students will enjoy hearing the best songs of 2018 or you can really throw it back and play a mash-up of songs from when they were "little."

The point of the quote is that grit cannot exist without the presence of both passion and perseverance. Explain that you are going to explore each of these in a balanced and fun way over the course of the year. You can also ask students to explain what passion and perseverance mean to them, and what other words they think of when they hear "grit." This will get the ball rolling for future activities.

In her research, Angela Duckworth (2016) found that grit was a better predictor of success than IQ. Explain that this is great news because we cannot dramatically change our IQ, but we can decide to push through challenges and pursue our interests – and those decisions will likely be the difference between those of us who are successful and those who are not. This also means that being smart is not the only thing that matters to being successful. What does matter is how hard we work.

Explain to students that you will be asking them throughout the year to share their research, fun facts, and ideas. We want them to understand that the reason for this is because we want to be able to springboard off the ideas of our peers. This is what community is all about and will allow us to see our connectedness.

When we are curious, we become interested in something. When we are interested in something, we are committed to learning more about it, which is when that "thing" becomes a passion. You can then explain to students that we are going to be cultivating curiosity regularly this year with the ultimate goal that everyone in the class can identify personal and academic passions.

We hear a lot of voices throughout the day, but the one that is the most powerful (because we hear it the most and because we can control it) is the one in our heads. So, we must train this voice to lift us up and be encouraging, especially when we are dealing with something difficult. You can use this as an opportunity to share a time when you had to reframe your thoughts to be more positive or encouraging. We want students to understand that it is not easy, but it can be done.

The most important word in this statement is CHOICE. Things are going to inevitably be difficult, but we have a choice. Do we keep moving forward or do we give up? Perseverance is making the decision to keep moving forward and it is incredibly important to the cultivation of grit.

$$\text{TALENT} \times \text{EFFORT}^2 = \text{ACHIEVEMENT}$$

I am bringing back some algebra here, so stick with me. I suggest that you start this discussion by writing these equations on the board. Then walk students through what they mean.

Talent x Effort = Skill → This means that when you have a talent (like basketball) and you apply some effort (like daily practice), the talent generally turns into a skill.

Skill x Effort = Achievement → This means that when you take that skill and add even more effort (like joining a team), the skill turns into achievement. If you combine these two equations, you get this simplified equation:

Talent x Effort^2 = Achievement → This means that effort counts twice when you want to achieve something (Duckworth, 2016). It counts more than talent and more than skill. And that, my friends, is incredibly life-changingly powerful.

Just like brushing our teeth every morning is a habit, working hard is a habit. If we work hard every single day in every single thing, that just becomes what we do. It is no longer a choice – it is just part of who we are. So that is why we have to train ourselves to give 100% effort to everything, even if we don't want to.

Ask students if they have wondered why passion is such an important piece to being gritty. Talk to them about a time when you had a goal but wanted to quit. Maybe you wanted to run a marathon. At some point in your training, you wanted to quit, but you did not. Why? Because you had a strong desire to finish what you started, to not let yourself down, and to see if you could do it.

All of this talk about grit and passion is really just getting to the heart of our "why." Why do we make the choices we make? Why are we doing what we are doing? It is really important that we know our "why" because this is what will guide us to living our best lives.

What does it mean to either win or learn? We want students to understand that winning is great, but if they don't win, it can still be a good experience. Everything they do is an opportunity to learn more about their likes, dislikes, strengths, and weaknesses.

Just because something is hard does not mean that it is not meant for us. In fact, if we think about the things that we are most proud of accomplishing, we will realize that those were not easy. We also call these productive successes. This entire unit on grit is designed to build up our capacity to understand ourselves so that we increase our chances of being successful. This is a great song by Tish Melton and Brandi Carlile (2021) called "We can do hard things": www.youtube.com/watch?v=vdm0Qz08ryo.

Recommended Order of Activities

I organized this book by topic, but it is really more beneficial to weave in and out of topics. For instance, we need to constantly revisit our goals so that they stay at the forefront of our minds. It does us no good to set a goal at the beginning of the year and then never think about it again. Instead, we should continue to think about and adjust them all year. I created this recommended order to provide you a structure for the "weaving in and out" that I am suggesting. I organized them by months to help with your lesson plans, but feel free to adjust and personalize to best meet your needs.

August	
Name of Activity	Corresponding Chapter
Steve Chen Profile	7
Gratitudes	5
I Wonder …	3
GRIT Acrostic	1
The Grit Quiz	1
Did You Know???	3
Big 10 Challenge	6
Why Does Grit Matter?	8
September	
Super Stretch Goals	2
I Used to Wonder …	3
Breaking down the Academic SSG	2
Patricia Medici Profile	7
Talent Brainstorm	6
Success in 20 Years	6
From Talent to Success	6
Road Map to Super Stretch Goal Success	6
October	
Challenges Faced	4
Self-Discipline	4
Breaking down the Personal SSG	2
Values	7
Cordelia Cranshaw Profile	7
Obstacle Brainstorm	4
SWOT Analysis	1
I Wonder …	3

November	
Problem Finding	7
My Favorites	6
Moving On	4
I Used to Wonder …	3
How I Want to Live My Life	8
Jennifer Lashbrook Profile	7
December	
Rethinking Failure	4
Productive and Unproductive Successes	4
Kid President Profile	7
Productive and Unproductive Failures	4
January	
Evaluating the Personal SSG	2
I Wonder …	3
Evaluating the Academic SSG	2
Jason Lester Profile	7
Grit and Growth Mindset	1
Distractions	4
February	
Ariana Grande Profile	7
I did it!	2
Feeling Like a Winner	2
Turning Skills into Achievements	6
Act Like a Winner	5
Practice Optimism	5
I Used to Wonder …	3
Connecting Interests	6
March	
Research Ideas	3
You Choose!	7
I Wonder …	3
Owning Your Power	1
Attitude of Gratitude	5
Not a Pretzel	8
My Inquiring Mind	3
Did You Know???	3
April	
Extrinsic Motivation	4
SWOT Review	1
Gunner Gillett Profile	7
Intrinsic Motivation	4
I Used to Wonder …	3

Failure ≠ Self-Worth	4
Reporting My Research	6
You Are the Captain!	5
May	
I Wonder …	3
I've Learned about Myself	5
Sucheta Kripalani Profile	7
I Need …	5
What Do I Stand For?	8
Turning Beliefs into Action!	8
June	
I Used to Wonder …	3
Benjamin "Kickz" Kapelushnik Profile	7
Thank You	5
Changes in Grit	1
July	
You Choose!	7
I Wonder …	3
I Did It!	2
My Future is Bright!	2

Note. A weekly calendar is included in this resource book and is described in Chapter 2. I suggest that you copy and use this weekly with students throughout the year.

References

About (n.d.). *Jennifer Lashbrook*. www.jenniferlashbrook.com/about

Alberts, E. C. (2016, November 23). Rescue goat with anxiety only calms down in her duck costume. *The Dodo*. www.thedodo.com/rescue-goat-duck-costume-2107301918.html

Angelou, M. [@DrMayaAngelou]. (2013, May 17). *This is a beautiful day. I've never seen this one before* [Tweet]. Twitter. https://twitter.com/drmayaangelou/status/335465952969900032?lang=en

Archer, L., Dawson, E., DeWitt, J., Godec, S., King, H., Mau, A., Nomikou, E., & Seakins, A. (2017). Killing curiosity? An analysis of celebrated identity performances among teachers and students in nine London secondary science classrooms. *Science Education*, *101*(5), 741–764.

Ariana Grande (2021, October 8). In *Wikipedia*. https://en.wikipedia.org/wiki/Ariana_Grande.

Associated Press (2019, February 4). Ariana Grande sued by artist over "God is a Woman" video. *Billboard.com*. www.billboard.com/articles/news/8496534/ariana-grande-sued-artist-god-is-a-woman-video

Baldwa, S. (2020, November 25). Sucheta Kripalani: India's first woman chief minister, chartered her own independent course. *Indian Express*. https://indianexpress.com/article/gender/sucheta-kripalani-indias-first-woman-chief-minister-chartered-her-own-independent-course-5111688/.

Before they were famous. Retrieved from www.alexanderjarvis.com/before-they-were-famous-15-startup-pivot-to-fame-8-youtube/

Benjamin Kapelushnik (2021, September 2). In *Wikipedia*. https://en.wikipedia.org/wiki/Benjamin_Kapelushnik.

Bhasker, J., Ruess, N., Dost, A., &. Antonoff, J. (2012). Some nights [Recorded by fun.]. On *Some Nights* [Album]. Fueled by Ramen, Atlantic (2011).

Biography.com Editors. (2021, May 19). Steve Chen biography. *The Biography.com Website* . www.biography.com/business-figure/steve-chen

Bustillo, D. (n.d.). 21 things you don't know about Ariana Grande. *Zimbio*. www.zimbio.com/21+Things+You+Don't+Know+About+Ariana+Grande.

Carnevale, A. P., Hanson, A. R., & Gulish, A. (2013). Failure to Launch: Structural Shift and the New Lost Generation. *Georgetown University Center on Education and the Workforce*.

Chen, S. (2021, July). *The Immigrant Learning Center*. www.ilctr.org/entrepreneur-hof/steve-chen/

Collier, R. (2009). *Riches within your reach!* The Penguin Group.

Deci, E. L., Koestner, R., & Ryan, R. M. (2001). Extrinsic rewards and intrinsic motivation in education: Reconsidered once again. *Review of Educational Research*, *71*(1), 1–27.

Doran, G. T. (1981). There's a S.M.A.R.T. way to write management goals and objectives. *Management Review*, *70*, 35–36.

Dredge, S. (2016, March 16). YouTube was meant to be a video-dating website. *The Guardian*. www.theguardian.com/technology/2016/mar/16/youtube-past-video-dating-website.

Dweck, C. S. (2007). *Mindset: The new psychology of success*. Ballantine Books.

Duckworth, A. L. (2016). *Grit: The power of passion and perseverance*. Scribner Book Company.

Duckworth, A. L. & Eskreis-Winkler, L. (2013, March 29). True grit. *Association for Psychological Science*. www.psychologicalscience.org/observer/true-grit?utm_source=socialmedia&utm_medium=sociallinks&utm_campaign=twitter

Duckworth, A. L., Peterson, C., Matthews, M. D., & Kelly, D. R. (2007). Grit: perseverance and passion for long-term goals. *Journal of Personality and Social Psychology*, *92*(6), 1087. doi: 10.1037/0022-3514.92.6.1087

Duckworth, A. L. & Quinn, P. D. (2009). Development and validation of the Short Grit Scale (GRIT–S). *Journal of Personality Assessment*, 91, 166–174. doi: 10.1080/00223890802634290

Duckworth, A. L. & Seligman, M. E. P. (2005). Self-discipline outdoes IQ in predicting academic performance of adolescents. *Psychological Science*, *16*(12), 939–944.

Editors, TheFamousPeople.com (n.d.) Robby Novak Biography. www.thefamouspeople.com/profiles/robby-novak-32687.php

Fry, R. (2016, May 24). For first time in modern era, living with parents edges out other living arrangements for 18–34-year-olds. *Pew Research Center*. www.pewresearch.org/social-trends/2016/05/24/for-first-time-in-modern-era-living-with-parents-edges-out-other-living-arrangements-for-18-to-34-year-olds/

Gregory, R. (2020, March 23). Carnivore vs. Vegan, Exogenous Ketones, and MetFlex Performance with Dr. Ryan Lowery (No. 7). [Audio podcast episode]. In *MetFlex and Chill*. https://metflexandchill.libsyn.com/

Hammitt, B. (2019, January 26). Happy birthday to the president that makes us smile. *The Unfinished Pyramid*. https://theunfinishedpyramid.com/2019/01/26/happy-birthday-to-the-president-that-makes-us-smile/

Hersh, R. H. & Merrow, J. (Eds.). (2005). *Declining by degrees: Higher education at risk*. Palgrave McMillan.

Hollis, R. (2019, July 13). I gave a keynote for 20,000 people in Indianapolis. It's the biggest crowd I've ever spoken in front of. It also – just so we're clear – took 15 years of work to get to a stage at this level. 15 years [Facebook status update.] Retrieved from https://m.facebook.com/TheChicSite/photos/i-gave-a-keynote-for-20000-people-in-indianapolis-its-the-biggest-crowd-ive-ever/10157153446096259/

Hosch, W. L. (2021, September 15). YouTube. *Encyclopedia Britannica*. www.britannica.com/topic/YouTube

Hyslop, G. (2016). The most basic thing millennials can do to impress their bosses. *Fortune*. Retrieved from https://fortune.com/2016/09/15/millennials-perseverance-boeing/.

Jason P. Lester (2021, October 8). In *Wikipedia*. https://en.wikipedia.org/wiki/Jason_P._Lester.

Kapur, M. (2016). Examining productive failure, productive success, unproductive failure, and unproductive success in learning. *Educational Psychologist, 51*(2), 289–299.

Kettle, B. & Ross, E. (2018). Strategies for engaging curious young minds in mathematics. *Educating Young Children: Learning and Teaching in the Early Childhood Years*, *24*(1), 33–34.

Marinova, P. (2016, September 15). 18 under 18: Meet the young innovators who are changing the world. *Fortune*. https://fortune.com/2016/09/15/18-entrepreneurs-under-18-teen-business/

Medici, P. (2015, August). The coolest animal you know nothing about … and how we can save it [Video]. *TED Conferences*. www.ted.com/talks/patricia_medici_the_coolest_animal_you_know_nothing_about_and_how_we_can_save_it?language=en.

Meet Jennifer Lashbrook (2019, January 31). *VoyageMIA*. http://voyagemia.com/interview/meet-jennifer-lashbrook/.

Melton, T. (2021). We can do hard things [Recorded by Tish Melton and Brandi Carlile].

Ocbazghi, E. (2018, January 5). Meet the 18-year-old entrepreneur making a fortune selling rare sneakers to celebrities. *Business Insider*. www.businessinsider.com/18-year-old-entrepreneur-makes-fortune-selling-rare-sneakers-to-celebrities-2018-1.

Patricia Medici (n.d.). Guardian of the lowland tapir. *Natural World Safaris*. www.naturalworldsafaris.com/natural-world-heroes/patricia-medici

Pestle Analysis Contributor (2015, March 5). Why SWOT analysis is essential in personal development. *Pestle Analysis*. https://pestleanalysis.com/swot-analysis-in-personal-development/.

Petrocchi, N. & Couyoumdjian, A. (2016). The impact of gratitude on depression and anxiety: the mediating role of criticizing, attacking, and reassuring the self. *Self and Identity*, *15*(2), 191–205. DOI: 10.1080/15298868.2015.1095794

Rathi, R. & Mishra, P. (2021, June 25). Jawed Karim biography: Co-founder of YouTube. *Startup Talky*. https://startuptalky.com/jawed-karim-youtube/.

Ris, E. W. (2015). Grit: A short history of a useful concept. *Journal of Educational Controversy, 10*(1). Retrieved from https://cedar.wwu.edu/jec/vol10/iss1/3/

Rubin, G. (2009, November 6). Act the way you want to feel. *Slate*. https://slate.com/human-interest/2009/11/act-the-way-you-want-to-feel.html

Salmansohn, K. (2016). *Think happy: Instant peptalks to boost positivity*. Ten Speed Press.

Sanguras, L. Y. (2018). *Raising Children with Grit: Parenting Passionate, Persistent, and Successful Kids* (1st ed.). Routledge. https://doi.org/10.4324/9781003237488

Singh, K. & Jha, S. D. (2008). Positive and negative affect, and grit as predictors of happiness and life satisfaction. *Journal of the Indian Academy of Applied Psychology*, *34*(2), 40–45.

Stokas, A. G. (2015). A genealogy of grit: Education in the new gilded age. *Educational Theory*, *65*(5), 513–528. https://doi.org/10.1111/edth.12130

Sucheta Kripalani (2021, September 14). In *Wikipedia*. https://en.wikipedia.org/wiki/Sucheta_Kripalani.

The John Maxwell Company (2011, August 3). To get back to the future, take care of today. *John C. Maxwell*. www.johnmaxwell.com/blog/to-get-back-to-the-future-take-care-of-today/

Warley, S. (2016). To find your passion, follow your curiosity. *Prsuit*. https://prsuit.com/find-your-passion-follow-your-curiosity/

Who is Cordelia Cranshaw? (n.d.). *YSocialWork*. https://ysocialwork.careers/who-is-cordelia-cranshaw/.

Witvliet, C. V., Richie, F. J., Root Luna, L. M., & Van Tongeren, D. R. (2019). Gratitude predicts hope and happiness: A two-study assessment of traits and states. *The Journal of Positive Psychology*, *14*(3), 271–282. DOI: 10.1080/17439760.2018.1424924

Wolters, C. A. & Hussain, M. (2015). Investigating grit and its relations with college students' self-regulated learning and academic achievement. *Metacognition and Learning*, *10*(3), 293–311.

YouTube (2021, October 13). In *Wikipedia*. https://en.wikipedia.org/wiki/YouTube.

9 781646 322176